50 Mexican Restaurant Dessert Recipes for Home

By: Kelly Johnson

Table of Contents

- Flan
- Churros
- Tres Leches Cake
- Arroz con Leche (Rice Pudding)
- Buñuelos
- Horchata
- Pan de Elote (Cornbread)
- Cajeta (Caramel Sauce)
- Empanadas de Manzana (Apple Empanadas)
- Pastel de Tres Leches
- Chocolate Abuelita Cake
- Mexican Wedding Cookies
- Capirotada (Mexican Bread Pudding)
- Gelatina (Mexican Gelatin Dessert)
- Conchas (Mexican Sweet Bread)
- Flan Napolitano
- Chocoflan (Impossible Cake)
- Paletas (Mexican Popsicles)
- Pan de Muerto (Day of the Dead Bread)
- Tequila Lime Pie
- Natilla (Custard)
- Cochinita Pibil Cake
- Dulce de Leche Cake
- Mantecada (Mexican Muffins)
- Capullo (Mexican Strawberry Cake)
- Molten Chocolate Lava Cake
- Tamales de Dulce (Sweet Tamales)
- Atole de Chocolate (Chocolate Atole)
- Mexican Coconut Cake
- Flan de Coco (Coconut Flan)
- Chocolate Mexicano Truffles
- Mexican Wedding Cake Balls

- Guava Paste and Cheese Dessert
- Pan de Calabaza (Pumpkin Bread)
- Sweet Corn Cake
- Chocoflan with Kahlúa
- Dulce de Leche Flan
- Mango with Tajín
- Piñata Cupcakes
- Mexican Hot Chocolate Cupcakes
- Mexican Rice Pudding with Cinnamon
- Pecan Pralines with Mexican Chocolate
- Mexican Cinnamon Rolls
- Churro Cheesecake
- Sweet Potato Flan
- Horchata Ice Cream
- Mexican Hot Chocolate Cake
- Vanilla Mexican Flan
- Plantain Fritters
- Strawberry Horchata Popsicles

Flan

Ingredients

For the Caramel:

- 1 cup granulated sugar
- 1/4 cup water

For the Flan:

- 1 can (14 oz) sweetened condensed milk
- 1 can (12 oz) evaporated milk
- 4 large eggs
- 1 tablespoon vanilla extract
- Pinch of salt

Instructions

1. **Prepare the Caramel:**
    - In a medium saucepan, combine the sugar and water. Cook over medium heat, stirring occasionally, until the sugar dissolves and the mixture turns a deep amber color (about 8-10 minutes).
    - Immediately pour the caramel into the bottom of a 9-inch round cake pan or flan mold, swirling to coat the bottom evenly. Be careful as the caramel is extremely hot.
2. **Prepare the Flan Mixture:**
    - Preheat your oven to 350°F (175°C).
    - In a large mixing bowl, whisk together the eggs, sweetened condensed milk, evaporated milk, vanilla extract, and a pinch of salt until smooth and well combined.
    - Strain the mixture through a fine-mesh sieve into another bowl to remove any lumps or bubbles.
3. **Bake the Flan:**
    - Pour the flan mixture over the set caramel in the prepared pan.
    - Place the pan in a larger baking dish or roasting pan. Add hot water to the larger pan to create a water bath (the water should come about halfway up the sides of the flan pan).
    - Bake for 50-60 minutes, or until the flan is set and a knife inserted into the center comes out clean.
4. **Cool and Serve:**
    - Remove the flan from the oven and let it cool to room temperature. Then refrigerate for at least 4 hours or overnight.

- To serve, run a knife around the edges of the flan to loosen it. Place a serving plate over the top of the pan, then carefully invert to release the flan onto the plate. The caramel will flow over the flan as a sauce.

Enjoy your homemade Flan!

Churros

Ingredients

For the Churros:

- 1 cup water
- 2 tablespoons granulated sugar
- 1/2 teaspoon salt
- 1/4 cup unsalted butter
- 1 cup all-purpose flour
- 3 large eggs
- Vegetable oil (for frying)

For the Cinnamon Sugar Coating:

- 1/2 cup granulated sugar
- 1 tablespoon ground cinnamon

Instructions

1. **Prepare the Churro Dough:**
    - In a medium saucepan, combine the water, sugar, salt, and butter. Bring to a boil over medium heat, stirring occasionally, until the butter is melted and the mixture is bubbling.
    - Remove the saucepan from the heat. Stir in the flour all at once, mixing vigorously until the dough comes together and pulls away from the sides of the pan.
    - Let the dough cool for about 5 minutes. Once it's cool enough to handle, stir in the eggs one at a time, mixing well after each addition. The dough should be smooth and slightly sticky.
2. **Prepare the Cinnamon Sugar Coating:**
    - In a small bowl, mix together the granulated sugar and ground cinnamon. Set aside.
3. **Fry the Churros:**
    - Heat about 2 inches of vegetable oil in a deep skillet or frying pan over medium-high heat. The oil should reach 350°F (175°C).
    - Fit a piping bag or a large resealable plastic bag with a large star-shaped piping tip. Fill the bag with the churro dough.
    - Carefully pipe strips of dough (about 4-6 inches long) into the hot oil. You can use scissors to cut the dough off the piping bag. Fry the churros in batches, avoiding overcrowding the pan. Cook for about 2-3 minutes per side, or until golden brown and crispy.

- Use a slotted spoon to transfer the fried churros to a paper towel-lined plate to drain excess oil.
4. **Coat with Cinnamon Sugar:**
    - While the churros are still warm, roll them in the cinnamon sugar mixture until fully coated.
5. **Serve:**
    - Serve the churros warm, ideally with a side of chocolate sauce or dulce de leche for dipping.

Enjoy your homemade churros!

Tres Leches Cake

Ingredients

For the Cake:

- 1 cup all-purpose flour
- 1 1/2 teaspoons baking powder
- 1/4 teaspoon salt
- 1/2 cup unsalted butter (room temperature)
- 1 cup granulated sugar
- 4 large eggs
- 1 teaspoon vanilla extract
- 1/2 cup whole milk

For the Milk Soak:

- 1 can (14 oz) sweetened condensed milk
- 1 can (12 oz) evaporated milk
- 1/2 cup whole milk

For the Whipped Cream Topping:

- 1 cup heavy cream
- 2 tablespoons granulated sugar
- 1 teaspoon vanilla extract

Instructions

1. **Prepare the Cake:**
   - Preheat your oven to 350°F (175°C). Grease and flour a 9x13-inch baking dish.
   - In a medium bowl, whisk together the flour, baking powder, and salt. Set aside.
   - In a large bowl, beat the butter and sugar together with an electric mixer on medium speed until light and fluffy (about 3 minutes).
   - Add the eggs one at a time, beating well after each addition. Mix in the vanilla extract.
   - Gradually add the flour mixture to the butter mixture, alternating with the whole milk. Begin and end with the flour mixture, mixing just until combined.
   - Pour the batter into the prepared baking dish and spread it evenly. Bake for 25-30 minutes, or until a toothpick inserted into the center comes out clean.
2. **Prepare the Milk Soak:**
   - While the cake is baking, in a medium bowl, whisk together the sweetened condensed milk, evaporated milk, and whole milk.

- Once the cake is done baking, remove it from the oven and let it cool in the pan for about 10 minutes.
- Use a fork or a skewer to poke holes all over the top of the warm cake. Slowly pour the milk mixture evenly over the cake, allowing it to soak in as you pour. Let the cake cool completely, then refrigerate for at least 4 hours, or overnight.

3. **Prepare the Whipped Cream Topping:**
   - In a large bowl, beat the heavy cream with an electric mixer on high speed until soft peaks form. Gradually add the sugar and vanilla extract, continuing to beat until stiff peaks form.
   - Spread the whipped cream evenly over the chilled cake.

4. **Serve:**
   - Decorate with fresh fruit or a sprinkle of cinnamon, if desired. Slice and serve chilled.

Enjoy your Tres Leches Cake!

Arroz con Leche (Rice Pudding)

Ingredients

- 1 cup long-grain white rice
- 2 cups water
- 4 cups whole milk
- 1 cup sugar
- 1 cinnamon stick
- 1 teaspoon vanilla extract
- 1/2 teaspoon ground cinnamon (optional, for garnish)
- 1/4 cup raisins (optional)
- 1/4 cup sweetened shredded coconut (optional)
- Pinch of salt

Instructions

1. **Cook the Rice:**
   - In a medium saucepan, combine the rice and water. Bring to a boil over medium-high heat.
   - Reduce the heat to low, cover, and simmer for about 15 minutes, or until the rice is tender and the water is absorbed.
2. **Prepare the Pudding Mixture:**
   - Add the milk, sugar, cinnamon stick, and a pinch of salt to the cooked rice. Stir to combine.
   - Bring the mixture to a gentle boil over medium heat, then reduce the heat to low. Cook, stirring frequently, for about 30-40 minutes, or until the mixture has thickened and the rice is very soft. If using raisins, add them during the last 10 minutes of cooking.
3. **Finish and Flavor:**
   - Stir in the vanilla extract.
   - Remove the cinnamon stick and discard it.
   - If you're adding shredded coconut, stir it in now and cook for an additional 5 minutes.
4. **Cool and Serve:**
   - Spoon the arroz con leche into serving dishes.
   - Let it cool slightly before serving. It can be enjoyed warm, at room temperature, or chilled.
   - If desired, sprinkle ground cinnamon on top before serving.

Tips

- For a creamier texture, you can substitute some of the milk with evaporated milk or add a bit of heavy cream.
- Arroz con leche can be refrigerated for up to 4 days. It may thicken as it sits; simply stir in a bit of milk to reach your desired consistency before serving.

Enjoy your homemade Arroz con Leche!

Buñuelos

Ingredients

For the Dough:

- 2 cups all-purpose flour
- 1/2 cup granulated sugar
- 1/2 teaspoon baking powder
- 1/4 teaspoon salt
- 1/2 cup unsalted butter (cold and cubed)
- 1 large egg
- 1/2 cup milk
- 1 teaspoon vanilla extract

For Frying:

- Vegetable oil (for frying)

For the Cinnamon Sugar Coating:

- 1/2 cup granulated sugar
- 1 tablespoon ground cinnamon

Instructions

1. **Prepare the Dough:**
   - In a large bowl, whisk together the flour, sugar, baking powder, and salt.
   - Cut in the cold, cubed butter using a pastry cutter or your fingers until the mixture resembles coarse crumbs.
   - In a separate bowl, whisk together the egg, milk, and vanilla extract.
   - Pour the wet ingredients into the dry ingredients and mix until a soft dough forms. If the dough is too sticky, add a bit more flour.
2. **Roll Out the Dough:**
   - Turn the dough out onto a lightly floured surface. Roll it out to about 1/8-inch thickness.
   - Use a round cutter (about 3-4 inches in diameter) or a glass to cut out circles of dough. You can also cut the dough into squares or other shapes if preferred.
3. **Fry the Buñuelos:**
   - Heat about 2 inches of vegetable oil in a deep skillet or frying pan over medium-high heat until it reaches 350°F (175°C).
   - Fry the dough pieces in batches, without overcrowding the pan, until they are golden brown and crispy, about 1-2 minutes per side.

- Use a slotted spoon to transfer the fried buñuelos to a paper towel-lined plate to drain excess oil.
4. **Coat with Cinnamon Sugar:**
    - In a shallow bowl, mix together the granulated sugar and ground cinnamon.
    - While the buñuelos are still warm, roll them in the cinnamon sugar mixture until evenly coated.
5. **Serve:**
    - Serve the buñuelos warm. They are delicious on their own or with a drizzle of honey or a side of chocolate sauce if you like.

Tips

- **Crispness:** Make sure the oil is hot enough before frying; otherwise, the buñuelos can absorb too much oil and become greasy.
- **Shaping:** For a traditional touch, you can make small, irregular shapes or use a rolling pin to make thin discs.

Enjoy your homemade buñuelos!

Horchata

Ingredients

- **1 cup long-grain white rice**
- **4 cups water**
- **1/2 cup milk** (whole milk or any milk alternative)
- **1/2 cup granulated sugar** (adjust to taste)
- **1 teaspoon ground cinnamon** (plus extra for garnish)
- **1 teaspoon vanilla extract**
- **1/4 cup slivered almonds** (optional, for extra flavor)
- **Ice** (for serving)

Instructions

1. **Soak the Rice:**
   - Rinse the rice under cold water until the water runs clear.
   - Place the rinsed rice in a bowl and cover it with 2 cups of water. Let it soak for at least 3 hours, or overnight for the best results.
2. **Blend the Mixture:**
   - Drain the rice, discarding the soaking water.
   - In a blender, combine the soaked rice, slivered almonds (if using), and 2 cups of fresh water. Blend until the mixture is smooth and creamy.
3. **Strain the Mixture:**
   - Strain the blended rice mixture through a fine-mesh sieve or cheesecloth into a large bowl or pitcher. Press on the solids to extract as much liquid as possible. Discard the solids.
4. **Flavor the Horchata:**
   - Stir in the milk, granulated sugar, ground cinnamon, and vanilla extract. Mix until the sugar is fully dissolved and the ingredients are well combined.
   - Taste and adjust the sweetness or cinnamon according to your preference.
5. **Chill and Serve:**
   - Refrigerate the horchata for at least 2 hours to chill and let the flavors meld.
   - Serve over ice and garnish with a sprinkle of ground cinnamon if desired.

Tips

- **Sweetness Level:** You can adjust the amount of sugar based on your taste preference. Add more sugar if you like it sweeter.
- **Spices:** For additional flavor, you can add a pinch of nutmeg or a few cloves when blending the mixture.

- **Vegan Option:** Substitute the milk with almond milk, oat milk, or another plant-based milk if you prefer a dairy-free version.

Enjoy your homemade horchata!

Pan de Elote (Cornbread)

Ingredients

- **2 cups fresh or frozen corn kernels** (about 2-3 ears of corn if using fresh)
- **1/2 cup unsalted butter** (softened)
- **1 cup granulated sugar**
- **4 large eggs**
- **1 cup all-purpose flour**
- **1 teaspoon baking powder**
- **1/2 teaspoon salt**
- **1/2 cup milk**
- **1 teaspoon vanilla extract**

Instructions

1. **Prepare the Corn:**
   - If using fresh corn, cut the kernels off the cob. If using frozen corn, thaw and drain it.
   - Blend the corn kernels in a blender or food processor until smooth. You should have about 1 1/2 to 2 cups of corn puree.
2. **Prepare the Batter:**
   - Preheat your oven to 350°F (175°C). Grease and flour a 9-inch round cake pan or a similar-sized baking dish.
   - In a large bowl, beat the softened butter and granulated sugar together until light and fluffy.
   - Add the eggs one at a time, beating well after each addition.
   - Stir in the corn puree and vanilla extract.
   - In a separate bowl, whisk together the flour, baking powder, and salt.
   - Gradually add the dry ingredients to the wet ingredients, mixing just until combined.
   - Stir in the milk until the batter is smooth and well combined.
3. **Bake the Cornbread:**
   - Pour the batter into the prepared baking pan and spread it evenly.
   - Bake in the preheated oven for 40-50 minutes, or until the top is golden brown and a toothpick inserted into the center comes out clean.
4. **Cool and Serve:**
   - Let the Pan de Elote cool in the pan for about 10 minutes before transferring to a wire rack to cool completely.
   - Serve warm or at room temperature. It's delicious on its own or with a dollop of whipped cream or a drizzle of honey.

Tips

- **Corn Flavor:** For a richer corn flavor, you can add a bit of cornmeal to the batter if desired.
- **Texture:** If you prefer a slightly crumbly texture, you can use a bit of cornmeal in place of some of the flour.
- **Variation:** Add a handful of fresh or frozen blueberries, or a sprinkle of cheese for a different twist.

Enjoy your homemade Pan de Elote!

Cajeta (Caramel Sauce)

Ingredients

- **4 cups goat's milk** (can substitute with whole milk, but goat's milk is traditional)
- **1 1/4 cups granulated sugar**
- **1/4 cup light corn syrup** (optional, helps to prevent crystallization)
- **1/4 teaspoon baking soda**
- **1/2 teaspoon vanilla extract**

Instructions

1. **Prepare the Ingredients:**
    - In a large, heavy-bottomed saucepan, combine the goat's milk, granulated sugar, and light corn syrup (if using).
2. **Cook the Mixture:**
    - Heat the mixture over medium heat, stirring frequently until the sugar is completely dissolved.
    - Once the sugar has dissolved, bring the mixture to a simmer. Reduce the heat to low and continue to simmer gently. Stir occasionally to prevent the milk from scorching on the bottom of the pan.
3. **Add Baking Soda:**
    - After about 30 minutes, add the baking soda. The mixture will foam up a bit, so be careful to avoid overflow.
    - Continue to cook, stirring frequently, until the mixture thickens and reduces to a syrupy consistency. This can take anywhere from 1 to 1.5 hours. The cajeta is done when it reaches a temperature of about 220°F (104°C) on a candy thermometer or when it coats the back of a spoon and drips off in thick ribbons.
4. **Finish the Sauce:**
    - Remove the pan from the heat and stir in the vanilla extract.
    - Allow the cajeta to cool slightly before transferring it to a clean jar or container. The sauce will thicken further as it cools.
5. **Store and Serve:**
    - Store the cajeta in the refrigerator for up to 2 weeks. It can be reheated gently in the microwave or on the stovetop before using.

Tips

- **Consistency:** If your cajeta is too thick after cooling, you can stir in a bit of milk to reach your desired consistency.
- **Flavor Variations:** For added flavor, consider adding a pinch of sea salt, a splash of rum, or a cinnamon stick during cooking.

- **Prevent Crystallization:** The corn syrup helps to prevent sugar crystallization, but if you prefer to avoid it, just make sure to keep stirring and maintain a gentle simmer to reduce crystallization.

Enjoy your homemade cajeta drizzled over ice cream, pancakes, or enjoyed straight from the jar!

Empanadas de Manzana (Apple Empanadas)

Ingredients

For the Dough:

- 2 1/2 cups all-purpose flour
- 1/2 cup granulated sugar
- 1 teaspoon baking powder
- 1/2 teaspoon salt
- 1/2 cup unsalted butter (cold and cubed)
- 1 large egg
- 1/4 cup milk (or more as needed)

For the Apple Filling:

- 3 medium apples (such as Granny Smith or Honeycrisp), peeled, cored, and diced
- 1/4 cup granulated sugar
- 1 teaspoon ground cinnamon
- 1 tablespoon all-purpose flour (to thicken the filling)
- 1 tablespoon lemon juice

For the Egg Wash:

- 1 large egg (beaten with 1 tablespoon water)

For the Sugar Coating (optional):

- 1/4 cup granulated sugar
- 1 teaspoon ground cinnamon

Instructions

1. **Prepare the Dough:**
    - In a large bowl, whisk together the flour, sugar, baking powder, and salt.
    - Cut in the cold, cubed butter using a pastry cutter or your fingers until the mixture resembles coarse crumbs.
    - In a small bowl, beat the egg and add the milk. Pour the wet ingredients into the dry ingredients and mix until a soft dough forms. If the dough is too dry, add more milk a tablespoon at a time.
    - Divide the dough into two discs, wrap in plastic wrap, and refrigerate for at least 30 minutes.
2. **Prepare the Apple Filling:**

- In a medium saucepan, combine the diced apples, sugar, cinnamon, flour, and lemon juice.
- Cook over medium heat, stirring occasionally, until the apples are tender and the mixture has thickened (about 5-7 minutes). Let the filling cool.

3. **Assemble the Empanadas:**
    - Preheat your oven to 375°F (190°C) and line a baking sheet with parchment paper.
    - On a lightly floured surface, roll out one disc of dough to about 1/8-inch thickness. Use a round cutter (about 4-5 inches in diameter) to cut out circles of dough.
    - Place a spoonful of apple filling in the center of each dough circle. Fold the dough over to form a half-moon shape and press the edges together to seal. You can use a fork to crimp the edges for a decorative touch.
    - Repeat with the remaining dough and filling.
4. **Apply Egg Wash and Bake:**
    - Brush the tops of the empanadas with the beaten egg wash.
    - If desired, mix the granulated sugar and cinnamon together and sprinkle over the empanadas.
    - Bake in the preheated oven for 20-25 minutes, or until the empanadas are golden brown and crisp.
5. **Cool and Serve:**
    - Allow the empanadas to cool slightly before serving.

Tips

- **Dough Texture:** If the dough is too crumbly, add a bit more milk. It should come together easily without being sticky.
- **Filling Variations:** You can add raisins, chopped nuts, or a bit of caramel sauce to the apple filling for added flavor.
- **Freezing:** These empanadas freeze well. Just freeze them unbaked on a baking sheet, then transfer to a zip-top bag. Bake from frozen, adding a few extra minutes to the baking time.

Enjoy your homemade empanadas de manzana!

Pastel de Tres Leches

Ingredients

For the Cake:

- 1 1/2 cups all-purpose flour
- 1 1/2 teaspoons baking powder
- 1/4 teaspoon salt
- 1/2 cup unsalted butter (room temperature)
- 1 cup granulated sugar
- 4 large eggs
- 1 teaspoon vanilla extract
- 1/2 cup whole milk

For the Milk Soak:

- 1 can (14 oz) sweetened condensed milk
- 1 can (12 oz) evaporated milk
- 1/2 cup whole milk

For the Whipped Cream Topping:

- 1 cup heavy cream
- 2 tablespoons granulated sugar
- 1 teaspoon vanilla extract

Instructions

1. **Prepare the Cake:**
    - Preheat your oven to 350°F (175°C). Grease and flour a 9x13-inch baking dish or a similar-sized pan.
    - In a medium bowl, whisk together the flour, baking powder, and salt. Set aside.
    - In a large bowl, beat the butter and sugar together with an electric mixer on medium speed until light and fluffy (about 3 minutes).
    - Add the eggs one at a time, beating well after each addition. Mix in the vanilla extract.
    - Gradually add the flour mixture to the butter mixture, alternating with the whole milk. Begin and end with the flour mixture, mixing just until combined.
    - Pour the batter into the prepared baking dish and spread it evenly. Bake for 25-30 minutes, or until a toothpick inserted into the center comes out clean.
2. **Prepare the Milk Soak:**

- While the cake is baking, in a medium bowl, whisk together the sweetened condensed milk, evaporated milk, and whole milk.
- Once the cake is done baking, remove it from the oven and let it cool in the pan for about 10 minutes.
- Use a fork or skewer to poke holes all over the top of the warm cake. Slowly pour the milk mixture evenly over the cake, allowing it to soak in as you pour. Let the cake cool completely, then refrigerate for at least 4 hours, or overnight.

3. **Prepare the Whipped Cream Topping:**
   - In a large bowl, beat the heavy cream with an electric mixer on high speed until soft peaks form. Gradually add the sugar and vanilla extract, continuing to beat until stiff peaks form.
   - Spread the whipped cream evenly over the chilled cake.

4. **Serve:**
   - Decorate with fresh fruit, a sprinkle of cinnamon, or a few mint leaves if desired. Slice and serve chilled.

Tips

- **Consistency:** The cake should be very moist but not soggy. If it seems too dry, you can carefully drizzle more of the milk mixture over it.
- **Flavor Additions:** You can add a splash of rum or a bit of citrus zest (like lime or orange) to the milk soak for additional flavor.
- **Presentation:** For a more festive presentation, you can top with berries or a fruit compote before serving.

Enjoy your homemade Pastel de Tres Leches!

Chocolate Abuelita Cake

Ingredients

For the Cake:

- 1 1/2 cups all-purpose flour
- 1 cup granulated sugar
- 1/2 cup unsweetened cocoa powder
- 1 1/2 teaspoons baking powder
- 1 1/2 teaspoons baking soda
- 1/2 teaspoon salt
- 1/2 cup unsalted butter (softened)
- 2 large eggs
- 1 cup milk
- 1/2 cup hot water
- 1 teaspoon vanilla extract
- 2 tablets (3 oz each) Chocolate Abuelita (crushed or finely chopped)

For the Chocolate Ganache:

- 1 cup heavy cream
- 8 oz semi-sweet chocolate (chopped)
- 1 tablespoon unsalted butter (optional, for extra shine)

For Garnish (optional):

- Whipped cream
- Chocolate shavings or grated Abuelita chocolate

Instructions

1. **Prepare the Cake:**
   - Preheat your oven to 350°F (175°C). Grease and flour two 8-inch round cake pans or one 9x13-inch baking dish.
   - In a large bowl, whisk together the flour, sugar, cocoa powder, baking powder, baking soda, and salt.
   - Add the softened butter, eggs, milk, and vanilla extract. Beat with an electric mixer on medium speed until smooth and well combined.
   - Dissolve the crushed Abuelita chocolate tablets in the hot water, stirring until fully melted and smooth. Allow to cool slightly.
   - Stir the melted chocolate mixture into the cake batter until well incorporated.

- Divide the batter evenly between the prepared cake pans or pour it into the baking dish. Smooth the top with a spatula.
  - Bake for 25-30 minutes for round pans or 35-40 minutes for a 9x13-inch dish, or until a toothpick inserted into the center comes out clean.
2. **Prepare the Chocolate Ganache:**
   - While the cake is cooling, heat the heavy cream in a saucepan over medium heat until it begins to simmer.
   - Remove from heat and add the chopped semi-sweet chocolate. Let it sit for a few minutes, then stir until smooth and glossy.
   - For extra shine, stir in the tablespoon of unsalted butter if using. Allow the ganache to cool slightly before using.
3. **Assemble the Cake:**
   - If using round pans, remove the cakes from the pans and place one layer on a serving plate.
   - Spread a layer of ganache over the first cake layer, then place the second layer on top.
   - Frost the top and sides of the cake with the remaining ganache. Smooth it out with a spatula or a knife.
4. **Garnish and Serve:**
   - Garnish with whipped cream, chocolate shavings, or grated Abuelita chocolate if desired.
   - Serve and enjoy!

Tips

- **Texture:** For a more pronounced chocolate flavor, you can add a bit of instant coffee or espresso powder to the cake batter.
- **Ganache:** If the ganache is too thick after cooling, you can reheat it gently to achieve the right consistency.
- **Storage:** The cake can be stored at room temperature for a few days or refrigerated for up to a week. The ganache will firm up in the refrigerator but can be softened by letting it sit at room temperature for a short while.

Enjoy your delicious Chocolate Abuelita Cake!

Mexican Wedding Cookies

Ingredients

- **1 cup unsalted butter** (softened)
- **1/2 cup granulated sugar**
- **2 cups all-purpose flour**
- **1 cup finely chopped pecans** (or walnuts, almonds, or your choice)
- **1/2 teaspoon vanilla extract**
- **1/4 teaspoon salt**
- **Powdered sugar** (for rolling)

Instructions

1. **Prepare the Dough:**
   - Preheat your oven to 350°F (175°C). Line a baking sheet with parchment paper or a silicone baking mat.
   - In a large bowl, beat the softened butter and granulated sugar together with an electric mixer on medium speed until light and fluffy.
   - Add the vanilla extract and mix until combined.
   - Gradually add the flour and salt, mixing on low speed until the dough just comes together.
   - Stir in the chopped pecans until evenly distributed.
2. **Shape the Cookies:**
   - Scoop tablespoon-sized portions of dough and roll them into balls. Place them about 1 inch apart on the prepared baking sheet. You can also shape them into crescent moons or any other shape you prefer.
3. **Bake the Cookies:**
   - Bake in the preheated oven for 12-15 minutes, or until the edges are lightly golden. The cookies should remain pale in color.
   - Remove from the oven and allow the cookies to cool on the baking sheet for about 5 minutes.
4. **Roll in Powdered Sugar:**
   - While still warm, carefully roll the cookies in powdered sugar to coat them thoroughly. Be gentle as the cookies are delicate and can break easily.
   - Allow the cookies to cool completely on a wire rack. Once cooled, roll them in powdered sugar again if desired.
5. **Store and Serve:**
   - Store the Mexican Wedding Cookies in an airtight container at room temperature for up to a week. They can also be frozen for longer storage.

Tips

- **Chop the Nuts Finely:** For a smoother texture, make sure to chop the nuts finely. You want them incorporated into the dough without large chunks.
- **Handle Gently:** The dough can be quite delicate, so handle the cookies gently to avoid breaking them.
- **Variations:** You can add a bit of cinnamon to the dough or use different nuts based on your preference.

Enjoy your homemade Mexican Wedding Cookies! They're perfect for sharing with family and friends during the holidays or any special occasion.

Capirotada (Mexican Bread Pudding)

Ingredients

For the Bread Pudding:

- **6 cups day-old bread** (such as French bread or bolillo), cut into cubes
- **1/2 cup unsalted butter** (for greasing the pan)
- **1 cup raisins**
- **1/2 cup chopped pecans** (or walnuts)
- **1/2 cup shredded cheese** (such as Monterey Jack or queso fresco, optional)
- **1/2 cup sliced almonds** (optional, for garnish)

For the Syrup:

- **1 cup packed brown sugar**
- **1 cup water**
- **1/2 cup honey**
- **1 cinnamon stick**
- **1 teaspoon ground cinnamon**
- **1/4 teaspoon ground cloves**
- **1/4 teaspoon ground allspice**
- **1 teaspoon vanilla extract**

Instructions

1. **Prepare the Bread:**
    - Preheat your oven to 350°F (175°C).
    - Spread the bread cubes in a single layer on a baking sheet. Toast in the preheated oven for about 10-15 minutes, or until golden brown and crisp. Set aside.
2. **Prepare the Syrup:**
    - In a medium saucepan, combine the brown sugar, water, honey, cinnamon stick, ground cinnamon, ground cloves, and ground allspice.
    - Bring to a boil over medium heat, stirring occasionally, until the sugar is completely dissolved and the syrup is slightly thickened (about 5-7 minutes).
    - Remove the saucepan from heat and stir in the vanilla extract. Discard the cinnamon stick.
3. **Assemble the Capirotada:**
    - Grease a 9x13-inch baking dish with the butter.
    - Arrange a layer of toasted bread cubes in the bottom of the prepared baking dish.
    - Sprinkle with some of the raisins, pecans, and shredded cheese if using.

- Repeat the layering process with the remaining bread, raisins, pecans, and cheese, finishing with a final layer of bread on top.
4. **Add the Syrup:**
    - Pour the warm syrup evenly over the layered bread, making sure to cover all the pieces. Gently press down on the bread with a spatula to help it absorb the syrup.
5. **Bake the Capirotada:**
    - Cover the baking dish with aluminum foil and bake in the preheated oven for 30 minutes.
    - Remove the foil and bake for an additional 15-20 minutes, or until the pudding is set and the top is golden brown.
6. **Garnish and Serve:**
    - If desired, sprinkle sliced almonds over the top during the last 5 minutes of baking for added crunch.
    - Allow the Capirotada to cool slightly before serving. It can be served warm or at room temperature.

Tips

- **Bread Choice:** Use day-old bread or slightly stale bread to prevent the pudding from becoming mushy.
- **Cheese:** The cheese adds a savory element to the sweet pudding, but it can be omitted if you prefer a sweeter version.
- **Add-Ins:** You can include other ingredients like chopped dried fruit, or a drizzle of extra honey or agave syrup if you like.

Enjoy your delicious homemade Capirotada!

Gelatina (Mexican Gelatin Dessert)

Ingredients

For the Gelatin Layers:

- **3 different flavors of gelatin** (each box is usually 3 oz or 85 g), such as strawberry, lime, and blueberry
- **1 can (14 oz) sweetened condensed milk**
- **1 cup boiling water (for each flavor)**
- **1 cup cold water (for each flavor)**
- **1 cup plain yogurt or sour cream** (optional, for creamier texture)

Instructions

1. **Prepare the First Layer:**
   - Dissolve one flavor of gelatin in 1 cup of boiling water, stirring until completely dissolved.
   - Stir in 1 cup of cold water.
   - Pour the mixture into a 9x13-inch baking dish or mold and refrigerate until fully set, about 1-2 hours.
2. **Prepare the Second Layer:**
   - Once the first layer is set, dissolve the second flavor of gelatin in 1 cup of boiling water, then stir in 1 cup of cold water.
   - Let the mixture cool slightly before gently pouring it over the set first layer. You can use a spoon to slowly pour the liquid over the back of it to prevent it from mixing with the first layer.
   - Refrigerate until fully set.
3. **Prepare the Third Layer:**
   - Dissolve the third flavor of gelatin in 1 cup of boiling water and stir in 1 cup of cold water. If using yogurt or sour cream, you can mix it in after the gelatin has dissolved and cooled slightly.
   - Pour the mixture over the set second layer as described before.
   - Refrigerate until the gelatin is completely set.
4. **Unmold and Serve:**
   - To unmold, dip the bottom of the mold briefly in warm water or place it in a shallow dish of warm water. This will help loosen the gelatin. Then invert the mold onto a serving plate.
   - Slice and serve chilled.

Tips

- **Texture Variation:** For a creamier dessert, you can mix some plain yogurt or sour cream into one or more of the gelatin layers after dissolving the gelatin but before setting.
- **Layering:** If you want to create a more intricate pattern, you can use cookie cutters to cut out shapes from one layer and arrange them in a new layer. Just be sure each layer is set before adding the next.
- **Flavors:** Feel free to mix and match flavors or use fruit juices instead of water for a different taste.

Enjoy your colorful and delightful Mexican Gelatina!

Conchas (Mexican Sweet Bread)

Ingredients

For the Dough:

- **4 cups all-purpose flour**
- **1/2 cup granulated sugar**
- **2 teaspoons instant yeast**
- **1 teaspoon salt**
- **1/2 cup unsalted butter** (softened)
- **1 cup warm milk** (110°F or 45°C)
- **2 large eggs**
- **1 teaspoon vanilla extract**

For the Topping:

- **1/2 cup unsalted butter** (softened)
- **1/2 cup granulated sugar**
- **1 cup all-purpose flour**
- **1/2 teaspoon baking powder**
- **1 teaspoon vanilla extract**
- **1 tablespoon cocoa powder** (optional, for a chocolate topping)

Instructions

1. **Prepare the Dough:**
    - In a large bowl or the bowl of a stand mixer, combine the flour, sugar, instant yeast, and salt.
    - Add the softened butter, warm milk, eggs, and vanilla extract. Mix until the dough begins to come together.
    - Knead the dough on a floured surface or with the stand mixer fitted with a dough hook, until it is smooth and elastic, about 8-10 minutes.
    - Place the dough in a lightly greased bowl, cover with a clean cloth or plastic wrap, and let it rise in a warm place until doubled in size, about 1-2 hours.
2. **Prepare the Topping:**
    - In a medium bowl, mix together the softened butter, sugar, flour, baking powder, and vanilla extract until well combined. If you're making a chocolate topping, divide the mixture in half and add cocoa powder to one half.
    - The topping should be thick and spreadable. If it's too soft, you can chill it briefly to firm it up.
3. **Shape the Conchas:**

- Once the dough has risen, punch it down and divide it into 12-15 equal pieces. Shape each piece into a ball and place them on a baking sheet lined with parchment paper, spaced a few inches apart.
- Let the dough balls rise again, covered loosely with a cloth, for about 30 minutes.

4. **Apply the Topping:**
   - Preheat your oven to 350°F (175°C).
   - Flatten each dough ball slightly, then use a sharp knife or a dough scraper to score a shell pattern into the topping. You can also use a cookie cutter or stencil for more defined patterns.
   - Gently spread the topping over each dough ball, making sure it covers the surface and the scored lines are visible.

5. **Bake the Conchas:**
   - Bake in the preheated oven for 15-20 minutes, or until the Conchas are golden brown and the topping is set and slightly cracked.
   - Allow to cool on a wire rack before serving.

Tips

- **Consistency of Topping:** If the topping is too runny, add a little more flour. If it's too thick, you can add a small amount of milk.
- **Flavor Variations:** Experiment with different flavors in the topping, such as adding spices or citrus zest.
- **Storage:** Conchas are best enjoyed fresh but can be stored in an airtight container at room temperature for a few days. They can also be frozen for longer storage.

Enjoy your homemade Conchas with a hot cup of coffee or hot chocolate!

Flan Napolitano

Ingredients

For the Caramel:

- 1 cup granulated sugar
- 1/4 cup water

For the Flan:

- 1 can (14 oz) sweetened condensed milk
- 1 can (12 oz) evaporated milk
- 4 large eggs
- 1 tablespoon vanilla extract
- 1/2 cup whole milk
- Pinch of salt

Instructions

1. **Prepare the Caramel:**
   - In a medium saucepan, combine the granulated sugar and water.
   - Cook over medium heat, stirring occasionally, until the sugar dissolves and turns a deep amber color. Be careful not to burn it.
   - Quickly pour the caramel into the bottom of a 9-inch round baking dish or a flan mold, tilting the pan to evenly coat the bottom. Set aside to cool and harden.
2. **Prepare the Flan Mixture:**
   - Preheat your oven to 350°F (175°C).
   - In a large bowl, whisk together the sweetened condensed milk, evaporated milk, whole milk, eggs, vanilla extract, and a pinch of salt until well combined and smooth. You can also use a blender for a smoother consistency.
3. **Bake the Flan:**
   - Pour the flan mixture over the hardened caramel in the baking dish.
   - Place the baking dish in a larger roasting pan. Pour hot water into the roasting pan until it reaches halfway up the sides of the flan dish to create a water bath (bain-marie).
   - Bake in the preheated oven for 50-60 minutes, or until the flan is set and a knife inserted into the center comes out clean.
4. **Cool and Unmold:**
   - Once baked, remove the flan from the oven and the water bath. Allow it to cool to room temperature, then refrigerate for at least 4 hours or overnight to fully set.

- To unmold, run a knife around the edges of the flan to loosen it. Invert a serving plate over the top of the baking dish, then carefully flip it over to release the flan onto the plate. The caramel will flow over the top as a sauce.
5. **Serve:**
    - Slice and serve chilled. Flan Napolitano is often enjoyed on its own, but it can also be garnished with fresh fruit or a dollop of whipped cream if desired.

Tips

- **Caramel:** Make sure to work quickly with the caramel as it hardens fast. If it gets too hard before pouring it into the pan, you can reheat it gently to soften it.
- **Texture:** For an extra smooth flan, strain the mixture through a fine-mesh sieve before baking to remove any bubbles or egg bits.
- **Water Bath:** Ensure the water in the roasting pan is hot when you add it to the oven for even baking.

Enjoy your delicious Flan Napolitano! It's a timeless dessert that never fails to impress.

Chocoflan (Impossible Cake)

Ingredients

For the Caramel:

- 1 cup granulated sugar
- 1/4 cup water

For the Flan:

- 1 can (14 oz) sweetened condensed milk
- 1 can (12 oz) evaporated milk
- 4 large eggs
- 1 tablespoon vanilla extract
- 1/2 cup whole milk
- Pinch of salt

For the Chocolate Cake:

- 1 1/2 cups all-purpose flour
- 1 cup granulated sugar
- 1/2 cup unsweetened cocoa powder
- 1 1/2 teaspoons baking powder
- 1 1/2 teaspoons baking soda
- 1/2 teaspoon salt
- 1/2 cup vegetable oil
- 1 cup hot water
- 2 large eggs
- 1 teaspoon vanilla extract

Instructions

1. **Prepare the Caramel:**
    - In a medium saucepan, combine the granulated sugar and water.
    - Cook over medium heat, stirring occasionally, until the sugar dissolves and turns a deep amber color. Be careful not to burn it.
    - Quickly pour the caramel into the bottom of a 9-inch round baking dish or flan mold, tilting the pan to evenly coat the bottom. Set aside to cool and harden.
2. **Prepare the Flan Mixture:**
    - Preheat your oven to 350°F (175°C).
    - In a large bowl or blender, combine the sweetened condensed milk, evaporated milk, whole milk, eggs, vanilla extract, and a pinch of salt. Blend until smooth.
3. **Prepare the Chocolate Cake Batter:**
    - In a large bowl, whisk together the flour, sugar, cocoa powder, baking powder, baking soda, and salt.

- Add the vegetable oil, hot water, eggs, and vanilla extract. Mix until smooth and well combined.
4. **Assemble the Cake:**
    - Pour the flan mixture over the hardened caramel in the baking dish.
    - Gently pour the chocolate cake batter over the flan mixture. The chocolate batter will float on top of the flan mixture, and during baking, the two will switch places.
5. **Bake the Chocoflan:**
    - Place the baking dish in a larger roasting pan. Pour hot water into the roasting pan until it reaches halfway up the sides of the baking dish to create a water bath (bain-marie).
    - Bake in the preheated oven for 60-70 minutes, or until a toothpick inserted into the center of the cake comes out clean.
6. **Cool and Unmold:**
    - Remove the Chocoflan from the oven and the water bath. Allow it to cool to room temperature, then refrigerate for at least 4 hours or overnight to fully set.
    - To unmold, run a knife around the edges of the Chocoflan to loosen it. Invert a serving plate over the top of the baking dish, then carefully flip it over to release the Chocoflan onto the plate. The caramel will flow over the top as a sauce.
7. **Serve:**
    - Slice and serve chilled. Chocoflan is a show-stopping dessert that is as delicious as it is impressive.

Tips

- **Caramel:** Be sure to work quickly with the caramel as it hardens fast. If it gets too hard before pouring it into the pan, you can gently reheat it to soften it.
- **Layering:** Pour the chocolate cake batter gently over the flan mixture to avoid disturbing the layers too much.
- **Cooling:** Make sure the Chocoflan is completely cooled and set before attempting to unmold it to prevent any breaking or collapsing.

Enjoy your delightful Chocoflan! It's a perfect combination of creamy flan and rich chocolate cake.

Paletas (Mexican Popsicles)

Ingredients

For Fruit Paletas:

- **4 cups fresh fruit** (such as strawberries, mangoes, or peaches), chopped
- **1/2 cup granulated sugar** (adjust to taste)
- **1/2 cup water** (or fruit juice)
- **1 tablespoon lemon or lime juice** (optional, for added brightness)

For Cream Paletas:

- **2 cups heavy cream**
- **1 cup sweetened condensed milk**
- **1 teaspoon vanilla extract**

Instructions

For Fruit Paletas:

1. **Prepare the Fruit:**
   - In a blender or food processor, combine the fresh fruit, granulated sugar, and water (or fruit juice). Blend until smooth. If using a fruit with a lot of seeds (like strawberries), you may want to strain the mixture through a fine-mesh sieve to remove seeds.
2. **Add Citrus (Optional):**
   - Stir in the lemon or lime juice if using. This adds a nice tang and can help balance the sweetness of the fruit.
3. **Pour into Molds:**
   - Pour the fruit mixture into popsicle molds. If you're using molds with sticks, insert the sticks according to the manufacturer's instructions.
4. **Freeze:**
   - Place the molds in the freezer and freeze for at least 4-6 hours, or until completely solid. For a smooth release, run warm water around the outside of the molds for a few seconds before removing the popsicles.

For Cream Paletas:

1. **Mix Ingredients:**
   - In a large bowl, whisk together the heavy cream, sweetened condensed milk, and vanilla extract until well combined.
2. **Pour into Molds:**

- Pour the cream mixture into popsicle molds. Insert the sticks.
3. **Freeze:**
   - Freeze for at least 4-6 hours, or until completely solid.

For Fruit and Cream Swirled Paletas:

1. **Prepare Both Mixtures:**
   - Make both the fruit and cream mixtures as described above.
2. **Layer in Molds:**
   - Spoon a small amount of fruit mixture into each mold, then add a layer of cream mixture. You can alternate layers or swirl them together for a marbled effect.
3. **Insert Sticks and Freeze:**
   - Insert the sticks and freeze for at least 4-6 hours, or until completely solid.

Tips

- **Customization:** You can experiment with different fruit combinations or add mix-ins like chocolate chips, nuts, or coconut flakes to your paletas.
- **Sweetness:** Adjust the amount of sugar based on the sweetness of the fruit and your personal preference. Some fruits are naturally sweeter and may need less sugar.
- **Mold Removal:** If you have trouble removing the paletas from the molds, briefly run warm water over the outside of the molds to help loosen them.

Enjoy your refreshing and homemade paletas! They're perfect for cooling off and indulging in delicious flavors.

Pan de Muerto (Day of the Dead Bread)

Ingredients

For the Dough:

- 4 cups all-purpose flour
- 1/2 cup granulated sugar
- 1/2 cup unsalted butter (softened)
- 1 cup warm milk (110°F or 45°C)
- 3 large eggs
- 1/4 cup orange juice
- 2 teaspoons active dry yeast
- 1 tablespoon orange zest (finely grated)
- 1/2 teaspoon ground cinnamon
- 1/2 teaspoon salt

For the Topping:

- 1/2 cup granulated sugar
- 1/4 cup unsalted butter (melted)
- 1 teaspoon ground cinnamon

For Decoration (Optional):

- Additional dough for bone shapes (optional)

Instructions

1. **Prepare the Dough:**
   - In a small bowl, dissolve the yeast in the warm milk and let it sit for about 5 minutes, or until frothy.
   - In a large bowl or the bowl of a stand mixer, combine the flour, sugar, and salt.
   - Add the softened butter, eggs, orange juice, and orange zest to the flour mixture. Pour in the yeast mixture.
   - Mix until the dough starts to come together, then knead on a floured surface or with the stand mixer fitted with a dough hook for about 8-10 minutes, until smooth and elastic.
   - Place the dough in a lightly greased bowl, cover with a clean cloth or plastic wrap, and let it rise in a warm place for about 1-2 hours, or until doubled in size.
2. **Shape the Bread:**

- Punch down the dough and turn it out onto a floured surface. Divide the dough into two portions: one larger portion for the main bread and a smaller portion for the decorations.
- Shape the larger portion into a round loaf and place it on a baking sheet lined with parchment paper.
- If making bone decorations, shape the smaller portion of dough into bone shapes (or small balls to resemble bones) and place them on top of the loaf. You can create a cross or a circle of bones on the loaf.

3. **Second Rise:**
   - Cover the shaped dough with a cloth and let it rise again for about 30-45 minutes, or until it has puffed up.
4. **Bake the Bread:**
   - Preheat your oven to 350°F (175°C).
   - Bake the Pan de Muerto for about 25-30 minutes, or until the bread is golden brown and sounds hollow when tapped on the bottom.
5. **Prepare the Topping:**
   - While the bread is baking, mix the granulated sugar and ground cinnamon in a bowl.
   - After the bread has finished baking, brush it with the melted butter and sprinkle the cinnamon-sugar mixture evenly over the top.
6. **Cool and Serve:**
   - Allow the Pan de Muerto to cool on a wire rack before serving.

Tips

- **Flavor Variations:** You can add other flavors to the dough, such as anise seeds or additional spices, to enhance the traditional taste.
- **Decoration:** The bone shapes can be tricky to get perfect, so don't worry if they don't look exactly like bones—just ensure they're well attached to the main loaf.
- **Storage:** Pan de Muerto is best enjoyed fresh but can be stored in an airtight container at room temperature for a few days. It can also be frozen for longer storage.

Enjoy your homemade Pan de Muerto! It's a special bread that brings a touch of tradition and celebration to the Day of the Dead festivities.

Tequila Lime Pie

Ingredients

For the Crust:

- 1 1/2 cups graham cracker crumbs
- 1/4 cup granulated sugar
- 1/2 cup unsalted butter (melted)

For the Filling:

- 1 can (14 oz) sweetened condensed milk
- 1 cup sour cream
- 1/2 cup fresh lime juice (about 4-5 limes)
- 2 tablespoons tequila
- 1 tablespoon lime zest (optional, for extra flavor)
- 4 large egg yolks

For the Topping:

- 1 cup heavy cream
- 2 tablespoons granulated sugar
- Lime zest or additional lime slices (for garnish)

Instructions

1. **Prepare the Crust:**
    - Preheat your oven to 350°F (175°C).
    - In a medium bowl, mix the graham cracker crumbs, sugar, and melted butter until well combined.
    - Press the mixture evenly into the bottom and up the sides of a 9-inch pie dish to form the crust.
    - Bake in the preheated oven for 8-10 minutes, or until lightly golden and set. Remove from the oven and let cool.
2. **Prepare the Filling:**
    - In a large bowl, whisk together the sweetened condensed milk, sour cream, lime juice, tequila, and lime zest (if using).
    - Add the egg yolks and whisk until the mixture is smooth and well combined.
    - Pour the filling into the cooled graham cracker crust.
3. **Bake the Pie:**
    - Bake in the preheated oven for 15-20 minutes, or until the filling is set and the edges are slightly puffed but the center is still slightly jiggly.

- Turn off the oven and let the pie cool in the oven with the door slightly ajar for about 1 hour. This helps prevent cracking. Afterward, refrigerate for at least 4 hours or until completely chilled and set.

4. **Prepare the Topping:**
    - In a medium bowl, beat the heavy cream and granulated sugar with an electric mixer until stiff peaks form.
    - Spread or pipe the whipped cream over the chilled pie.
5. **Garnish and Serve:**
    - Garnish with additional lime zest or lime slices, if desired.
    - Slice and serve chilled.

Tips

- **Tequila:** Use a good-quality tequila for the best flavor. You can also use flavored tequila for an additional twist.
- **Lime Juice:** Fresh lime juice is preferable for the best flavor, but bottled lime juice can be used in a pinch.
- **Whipped Cream:** For a smoother topping, you can also use store-bought whipped cream if you're short on time.

Enjoy your Tequila Lime Pie! It's a refreshing and indulgent dessert that adds a fun twist to the classic lime pie.

Natilla (Custard)

Ingredients

- **2 cups whole milk**
- **1 cup heavy cream**
- **3/4 cup granulated sugar**
- **3 large egg yolks**
- **2 tablespoons cornstarch**
- **1 teaspoon vanilla extract**
- **1 cinnamon stick** (optional)
- **1 tablespoon butter** (optional, for extra richness)

Instructions

1. **Heat the Milk and Cream:**
    - In a medium saucepan, combine the whole milk and heavy cream. If using a cinnamon stick, add it to the mixture.
    - Heat over medium heat until it begins to simmer. Do not let it boil. Once it's hot, remove it from the heat and discard the cinnamon stick if used. Let it cool slightly.
2. **Prepare the Egg Mixture:**
    - In a separate bowl, whisk together the egg yolks and granulated sugar until well combined and slightly pale.
    - In another small bowl, dissolve the cornstarch in a few tablespoons of cold milk to make a slurry.
3. **Combine and Cook:**
    - Gradually add the hot milk mixture to the egg yolk mixture, whisking constantly to temper the eggs and prevent curdling.
    - Pour the combined mixture back into the saucepan.
    - Cook over medium heat, whisking constantly, until the mixture thickens and reaches a custard-like consistency. This should take about 5-7 minutes. Do not let it boil, as it can cause the custard to curdle.
4. **Finish the Custard:**
    - Once thickened, remove the saucepan from the heat.
    - Stir in the vanilla extract and butter if using. The butter adds a nice richness to the custard.
    - Strain the custard through a fine-mesh sieve into a clean bowl to ensure it is smooth and to remove any lumps.
5. **Cool and Serve:**
    - Let the Natilla cool to room temperature. Once cooled, cover and refrigerate for at least 2 hours or until chilled and set.

- Serve chilled, either on its own or topped with a sprinkle of cinnamon or a dollop of whipped cream if desired.

Tips

- **Consistency:** If the Natilla is too thick after cooling, you can whisk in a little more milk to reach your desired consistency.
- **Flavor Variations:** For different flavors, you can add a splash of citrus zest, a few drops of almond extract, or a sprinkle of nutmeg.
- **Serving:** Natilla can be served in individual cups or dishes, making it easy for guests to enjoy.

Enjoy your homemade Natilla! It's a simple yet elegant dessert that's perfect for any occasion.

Cochinita Pibil Cake

Ingredients

For the Cochinita Pibil:

- **2 pounds pork shoulder or butt** (cut into chunks)
- **1/2 cup achiote paste**
- **1/2 cup orange juice**
- **1/4 cup white vinegar**
- **4 cloves garlic** (minced)
- **1 tablespoon dried oregano**
- **1 teaspoon ground cumin**
- **1 teaspoon ground black pepper**
- **1 teaspoon salt**
- **1 bay leaf**
- **2-3 banana leaves** (optional, for authentic flavor and wrapping)

For the Cake Layers (Cornmeal Base):

- **1 1/2 cups cornmeal**
- **1 1/2 cups all-purpose flour**
- **1/2 cup granulated sugar**
- **1 tablespoon baking powder**
- **1/2 teaspoon salt**
- **1/2 cup unsalted butter** (softened)
- **2 large eggs**
- **1 cup milk**
- **1/4 cup vegetable oil**
- **1 cup shredded cheese** (optional, for added flavor)

For the Assembly:

- **Sour cream or Mexican crema** (for spreading between layers)
- **Fresh cilantro** (chopped, for garnish)
- **Lime wedges** (for serving)

Instructions

1. **Prepare the Cochinita Pibil:**
    - In a large bowl, mix together the achiote paste, orange juice, vinegar, garlic, oregano, cumin, black pepper, and salt.

- Coat the pork chunks with the marinade mixture and let it marinate in the refrigerator for at least 2 hours or overnight for best flavor.
- If using banana leaves, heat them briefly over an open flame or in the oven to make them pliable, then line a baking dish with them.
- Preheat your oven to 300°F (150°C).
- Place the marinated pork and bay leaf in a roasting pan or Dutch oven. Cover tightly with foil (and banana leaves if using) and roast for 3-4 hours, or until the pork is tender and easily shredable.
- Once cooked, shred the pork with two forks and set aside. Discard any excess fat.

2. **Prepare the Cake Layers:**
    - Preheat your oven to 350°F (175°C). Grease and flour two 9-inch round cake pans.
    - In a large bowl, whisk together the cornmeal, flour, sugar, baking powder, and salt.
    - In another bowl, beat the softened butter until creamy. Add the eggs one at a time, beating well after each addition. Mix in the milk and vegetable oil.
    - Gradually add the dry ingredients to the wet ingredients, mixing until just combined. Fold in the shredded cheese if using.
    - Divide the batter evenly between the prepared cake pans and smooth the tops.
    - Bake in the preheated oven for 20-25 minutes, or until a toothpick inserted into the center of the cakes comes out clean. Allow to cool in the pans for 10 minutes before transferring to a wire rack to cool completely.

3. **Assemble the Cake:**
    - Once the cake layers are completely cooled, spread a layer of sour cream or Mexican crema on top of one cake layer.
    - Evenly spread a layer of shredded Cochinita Pibil over the sour cream.
    - Place the second cake layer on top and spread with more sour cream or Mexican crema. Top with additional Cochinita Pibil if desired.
    - Garnish with chopped fresh cilantro and serve with lime wedges.

Tips

- **Authenticity:** Using banana leaves adds authenticity and a subtle flavor, but you can also use foil if they're not available.
- **Layers:** Adjust the amount of Cochinita Pibil and sour cream between layers based on your preference.
- **Cheese:** The cheese in the cornmeal base adds a savory touch, but it's optional based on your taste preference.

Enjoy your unique Cochinita Pibil Cake, a delicious fusion of savory and sweet flavors that brings a touch of Mexican cuisine to a classic cake concept!

Dulce de Leche Cake

Ingredients

For the Cake:

- 2 1/2 cups all-purpose flour
- 2 1/2 teaspoons baking powder
- 1/2 teaspoon baking soda
- 1/2 teaspoon salt
- 1 cup unsalted butter (softened)
- 1 1/2 cups granulated sugar
- 4 large eggs
- 1 cup sour cream
- 1/2 cup whole milk
- 2 teaspoons vanilla extract

For the Dulce de Leche Filling and Frosting:

- 1 cup dulce de leche (store-bought or homemade)
- 1 cup heavy cream
- 1/2 cup powdered sugar
- 1 teaspoon vanilla extract

For Garnish (Optional):

- Whipped cream
- Caramel sauce
- Sea salt
- Chopped nuts or shaved chocolate

Instructions

1. **Prepare the Cake:**
   - Preheat your oven to 350°F (175°C). Grease and flour two 9-inch round cake pans.
   - In a medium bowl, whisk together the flour, baking powder, baking soda, and salt. Set aside.
   - In a large bowl or the bowl of a stand mixer, beat the softened butter and granulated sugar until light and fluffy.
   - Add the eggs one at a time, beating well after each addition.
   - Mix in the vanilla extract.

- Gradually add the flour mixture to the butter mixture in alternating batches with the sour cream and milk, beginning and ending with the flour mixture. Mix until just combined.
- Divide the batter evenly between the prepared cake pans and smooth the tops.
- Bake for 25-30 minutes, or until a toothpick inserted into the center of the cakes comes out clean.
- Allow the cakes to cool in the pans for 10 minutes before transferring to a wire rack to cool completely.

2. **Prepare the Dulce de Leche Filling and Frosting:**
    - In a large bowl, beat the heavy cream, powdered sugar, and vanilla extract until stiff peaks form.
    - Gently fold in the dulce de leche until fully combined. Be careful not to deflate the whipped cream too much.

3. **Assemble the Cake:**
    - Once the cakes are completely cooled, level the tops with a knife if necessary.
    - Place one cake layer on a serving plate or cake stand. Spread a generous amount of the dulce de leche filling and frosting over the top.
    - Place the second cake layer on top and frost the top and sides of the cake with the remaining dulce de leche frosting.
    - Smooth the frosting with a spatula or create swirls for a decorative effect.

4. **Garnish and Serve:**
    - Garnish with whipped cream, caramel sauce, a sprinkle of sea salt, or chopped nuts if desired.
    - Slice and serve. The cake can be stored in the refrigerator for several days.

Tips

- **Dulce de Leche:** If you're making homemade dulce de leche, make sure it's completely cooled before using it in the frosting.
- **Consistency:** If the frosting is too thick, you can gently fold in a bit more heavy cream to reach your desired consistency.
- **Flavor Additions:** For added flavor, you can mix in a bit of espresso powder or cocoa powder into the frosting, or layer the cake with fruit preserves.

Enjoy your Dulce de Leche Cake, a deliciously sweet and creamy treat that's sure to impress!

Mantecada (Mexican Muffins)

Ingredients

For the Mantecadas:

- 2 1/2 cups all-purpose flour
- 1 cup granulated sugar
- 1/2 cup unsalted butter (softened)
- 1 cup milk
- 2 large eggs
- 1 tablespoon baking powder
- 1/2 teaspoon salt
- 1 teaspoon vanilla extract
- 1/2 teaspoon ground cinnamon (optional)

For the Topping:

- 1/4 cup granulated sugar
- 1 teaspoon ground cinnamon (optional)

Instructions

1. **Preheat the Oven:**
   - Preheat your oven to 350°F (175°C). Line a muffin tin with paper liners or grease the cups.
2. **Prepare the Batter:**
   - In a medium bowl, whisk together the flour, baking powder, salt, and ground cinnamon (if using). Set aside.
   - In a large bowl or the bowl of a stand mixer, cream together the softened butter and granulated sugar until light and fluffy.
   - Add the eggs one at a time, beating well after each addition.
   - Mix in the vanilla extract.
   - Gradually add the dry ingredients to the wet ingredients, alternating with the milk, beginning and ending with the dry ingredients. Mix until just combined.
3. **Fill the Muffin Tin:**
   - Spoon the batter into the prepared muffin tin, filling each cup about 2/3 full.
4. **Prepare the Topping:**
   - In a small bowl, mix the granulated sugar and ground cinnamon (if using).
   - Sprinkle the sugar mixture evenly over the tops of the muffin batter.
5. **Bake the Mantecadas:**
   - Bake in the preheated oven for 18-22 minutes, or until a toothpick inserted into the center of a muffin comes out clean.

6. **Cool and Serve:**
    - Allow the mantecadas to cool in the tin for 5 minutes before transferring them to a wire rack to cool completely.

Tips

- **Butter:** Make sure the butter is softened to room temperature for the best texture.
- **Mixing:** Avoid over-mixing the batter to keep the mantecadas light and tender.
- **Customization:** You can add mix-ins like chocolate chips, nuts, or dried fruit for variation.
- **Storage:** Store mantecadas in an airtight container at room temperature for up to a week.

Enjoy your homemade mantecadas! They're perfect for a sweet breakfast, an afternoon snack, or as a treat to share with friends and family.

Capullo (Mexican Strawberry Cake)

Ingredients

For the Cake:

- 1 1/2 cups all-purpose flour
- 1 cup granulated sugar
- 1/2 cup unsalted butter (softened)
- 1 cup fresh strawberries (pureed)
- 1/2 cup milk
- 3 large eggs
- 1 tablespoon baking powder
- 1/4 teaspoon salt
- 1 teaspoon vanilla extract

For the Strawberry Frosting:

- 1/2 cup unsalted butter (softened)
- 2 cups powdered sugar
- 1/4 cup fresh strawberries (pureed)
- 1 tablespoon milk (if needed for consistency)
- 1 teaspoon vanilla extract

For Garnish (Optional):

- **Fresh strawberries** (sliced)
- **Mint leaves**

Instructions

1. **Prepare the Cake:**
    - Preheat your oven to 350°F (175°C). Grease and flour two 8-inch round cake pans.
    - In a medium bowl, whisk together the flour, baking powder, and salt. Set aside.
    - In a large bowl or the bowl of a stand mixer, cream together the softened butter and granulated sugar until light and fluffy.
    - Add the eggs one at a time, beating well after each addition.
    - Mix in the vanilla extract.
    - Gradually add the flour mixture to the butter mixture, alternating with the milk, beginning and ending with the flour mixture. Mix until just combined.
    - Fold in the pureed strawberries until evenly distributed.
    - Divide the batter evenly between the prepared cake pans and smooth the tops.

2. **Bake the Cake:**
    - Bake in the preheated oven for 25-30 minutes, or until a toothpick inserted into the center of the cakes comes out clean.
    - Allow the cakes to cool in the pans for 10 minutes before transferring them to a wire rack to cool completely.
3. **Prepare the Strawberry Frosting:**
    - In a large bowl, beat the softened butter until creamy.
    - Gradually add the powdered sugar, beating well after each addition.
    - Mix in the pureed strawberries and vanilla extract.
    - If the frosting is too thick, add a tablespoon of milk to reach your desired consistency.
4. **Assemble the Cake:**
    - Once the cakes are completely cooled, level the tops with a knife if necessary.
    - Place one cake layer on a serving plate or cake stand. Spread a layer of strawberry frosting over the top.
    - Place the second cake layer on top and frost the top and sides of the cake with the remaining strawberry frosting.
    - Garnish with fresh strawberry slices and mint leaves if desired.
5. **Serve:**
    - Slice and serve the cake. It's perfect with a cup of tea or coffee.

Tips

- **Strawberries:** Use fresh strawberries for the best flavor. If using frozen strawberries, make sure they are well-drained.
- **Frosting Consistency:** If the frosting is too runny, add a little more powdered sugar. If too thick, add a bit more milk.
- **Flavor Boost:** You can enhance the strawberry flavor with a touch of lemon zest or a splash of lemon juice in the cake batter or frosting.

Enjoy your Capullo, a beautiful and delicious strawberry cake that's sure to impress!

Molten Chocolate Lava Cake

Ingredients

For the Lava Cakes:

- **1/2 cup unsalted butter** (plus extra for greasing)
- **1 cup semi-sweet chocolate chips** or chopped chocolate
- **1 cup powdered sugar**
- **2 large eggs**
- **2 large egg yolks**
- **1 teaspoon vanilla extract**
- **1/2 cup all-purpose flour**
- **A pinch of salt**

For Serving (Optional):

- **Powdered sugar** (for dusting)
- **Vanilla ice cream** or **whipped cream**
- **Fresh berries** (like raspberries or strawberries)

Instructions

1. **Prepare the Ramekins:**
    - Preheat your oven to 425°F (220°C).
    - Grease four 6-ounce ramekins with butter and lightly dust them with flour or cocoa powder to prevent sticking.
2. **Make the Chocolate Mixture:**
    - In a medium microwave-safe bowl, melt the butter and chocolate together. Heat in 30-second intervals, stirring between each interval, until the mixture is smooth and fully melted. Alternatively, you can melt the butter and chocolate in a heatproof bowl over a pot of simmering water (double boiler method).
    - Stir in the powdered sugar until well combined.
3. **Add the Eggs:**
    - Whisk the eggs and egg yolks into the chocolate mixture until fully incorporated.
    - Mix in the vanilla extract.
4. **Add the Flour:**
    - Gently fold in the flour and a pinch of salt until just combined. Be careful not to overmix.
5. **Fill the Ramekins:**
    - Divide the batter evenly among the prepared ramekins.
6. **Bake the Cakes:**

- Bake in the preheated oven for 12-14 minutes, or until the edges are set and the center is still slightly jiggly.
- The key to the molten center is to not overbake; the center should be soft and gooey when you cut into it.

7. **Serve:**
    - Allow the cakes to cool in the ramekins for 1 minute. Carefully run a knife around the edges to loosen them, then invert the cakes onto individual plates.
    - Dust with powdered sugar and serve immediately with vanilla ice cream or whipped cream, and fresh berries if desired.

Tips

- **Chocolate:** Use high-quality chocolate for the best results. Semi-sweet chocolate chips or high-quality chocolate bars work well.
- **Ramekins:** Ensure the ramekins are well greased to help the cakes release easily.
- **Baking Time:** Keep an eye on the cakes as they bake. Oven temperatures vary, so you might need to adjust the baking time slightly.
- **Make-Ahead:** You can prepare the batter ahead of time, spoon it into the ramekins, cover, and refrigerate. When ready to bake, just add an extra minute or two to the baking time.

Enjoy your Molten Chocolate Lava Cake, a sumptuous treat that's perfect for any chocolate lover!

Tamales de Dulce (Sweet Tamales)

Ingredients

For the Tamales:

- **2 cups masa harina** (corn flour for tamales)
- **1/2 cup granulated sugar**
- **1 teaspoon baking powder**
- **1/2 teaspoon salt**
- **1/2 cup unsalted butter** (softened)
- **1 cup milk** (or more as needed)
- **1 teaspoon vanilla extract**
- **1/2 teaspoon ground cinnamon** (optional)
- **1/2 cup raisins** (optional)
- **1/2 cup chopped nuts** (optional)

For Steaming:

- **Corn husks** (soaked in warm water for 30 minutes to 1 hour)

Instructions

1. **Prepare the Corn Husks:**
    - Soak the corn husks in warm water for 30 minutes to 1 hour, until they become pliable. Drain and pat dry.
2. **Prepare the Tamale Dough:**
    - In a large bowl, combine the masa harina, sugar, baking powder, salt, and ground cinnamon (if using).
    - Add the softened butter and mix until the mixture resembles coarse crumbs.
    - Gradually add the milk and vanilla extract, mixing until the dough is soft and pliable. You might need to adjust the amount of milk to get the right consistency. The dough should be moist but not too runny.
3. **Add Optional Ingredients:**
    - Fold in the raisins and chopped nuts if using.
4. **Assemble the Tamales:**
    - Spread a small amount of masa dough onto the center of each corn husk, leaving space at the edges. The layer of dough should be about 1/4 inch thick.
    - Fold the sides of the husk over the masa to form a packet. Fold up the bottom of the husk to secure the tamale.
    - Repeat until all the masa dough is used.
5. **Steam the Tamales:**

- Arrange the tamales upright in a large steamer or tamale pot. If necessary, use additional corn husks or a dishcloth to help keep the tamales upright and prevent them from falling over.
- Cover the tamales with a damp cloth or additional corn husks.
- Steam over medium heat for 1 to 1 1/2 hours, or until the masa is fully cooked and the tamales easily separate from the husks. Check occasionally and add water to the steamer as needed.

6. **Serve:**
   - Allow the tamales to cool slightly before serving. They can be enjoyed warm or at room temperature.

Tips

- **Masa Consistency:** The masa should be soft and spreadable. If it's too dry, add a bit more milk; if too wet, add a little more masa harina.
- **Flavor Variations:** Experiment with different flavors by adding ingredients like cocoa powder, fruit preserves, or coconut flakes to the dough.
- **Storage:** Tamales can be stored in an airtight container in the refrigerator for up to a week or frozen for up to 3 months. Reheat by steaming or microwaving.

Sweet Tamales are a delicious and versatile treat that can be customized to your liking. Enjoy making and sharing these delightful tamales!

Atole de Chocolate (Chocolate Atole)

Ingredients

- **4 cups whole milk**
- **1/2 cup masa harina** (corn flour for tortillas or tamales)
- **1/2 cup sugar** (adjust to taste)
- **1/2 cup cocoa powder** (or 3.5 oz of Mexican chocolate, chopped)
- **1/4 cup water**
- **1/2 teaspoon vanilla extract**
- **1/4 teaspoon ground cinnamon** (optional)
- **A pinch of salt**

Instructions

1. **Prepare the Chocolate Mixture:**
    - In a small bowl, mix the cocoa powder (or chopped Mexican chocolate) with the 1/4 cup of water to create a smooth paste. If using Mexican chocolate, you might need to melt it slightly to mix well.
2. **Make the Atole Base:**
    - In a large saucepan, combine the milk and masa harina. Whisk well to ensure that the masa harina is fully incorporated and no lumps remain.
3. **Cook the Atole:**
    - Place the saucepan over medium heat and cook the mixture, stirring constantly, until it starts to thicken. This should take about 5-7 minutes. Be sure to keep stirring to prevent the masa from sticking to the bottom of the pan.
4. **Add the Chocolate:**
    - Stir in the chocolate paste (or melted Mexican chocolate) and continue to cook, stirring constantly, until the chocolate is fully melted and incorporated into the mixture.
5. **Sweeten and Flavor:**
    - Add the sugar, vanilla extract, ground cinnamon (if using), and a pinch of salt. Stir until the sugar is dissolved and the atole is smooth and well combined.
6. **Serve:**
    - Remove from heat and ladle the Atole de Chocolate into mugs. Serve warm.

Tips

- **Consistency:** If the atole is too thick, you can thin it out by adding more milk. If it's too thin, cook it a bit longer to thicken.
- **Mexican Chocolate:** Mexican chocolate has a unique flavor due to the addition of spices and sugar. If you don't have it, cocoa powder can be used as a substitute, though the flavor will be slightly different.
- **Flavors:** For extra flavor, you can add a pinch of nutmeg, or a splash of liqueur like Kahlúa or Baileys, or top with whipped cream for a special touch.

Atole de Chocolate is a deliciously comforting drink that's perfect for enjoying with a sweet bread or pastry. It's especially enjoyable during colder months or as a special treat for breakfast. Enjoy!

Mexican Coconut Cake

Ingredients

For the Cake:

- **1 1/2 cups all-purpose flour**
- **1 cup granulated sugar**
- **1/2 cup unsalted butter** (softened)
- **1 cup canned coconut milk** (full-fat for best results)
- **3 large eggs**
- **1 teaspoon vanilla extract**
- **1 teaspoon baking powder**
- **1/2 teaspoon baking soda**
- **1/4 teaspoon salt**
- **1 cup shredded coconut** (sweetened or unsweetened, as per your preference)

For the Coconut Frosting:

- **1/2 cup unsalted butter** (softened)
- **1 cup coconut cream** (from a can of coconut milk or heavy cream)
- **2 cups powdered sugar**
- **1 teaspoon vanilla extract**
- **1/2 cup shredded coconut** (for garnish, optional)

For Garnish (Optional):

- **Toasted shredded coconut**
- **Fresh coconut flakes**

Instructions

1. **Prepare the Cake:**
    - Preheat your oven to 350°F (175°C). Grease and flour two 8-inch round cake pans or one 9x13-inch pan.
    - In a medium bowl, whisk together the flour, baking powder, baking soda, and salt. Set aside.
    - In a large bowl or the bowl of a stand mixer, cream the softened butter and granulated sugar until light and fluffy.
    - Add the eggs one at a time, beating well after each addition. Mix in the vanilla extract.
    - Gradually add the dry ingredients to the butter mixture, alternating with the coconut milk. Begin and end with the dry ingredients. Mix until just combined.

- Fold in the shredded coconut.
- Divide the batter evenly between the prepared cake pans or pour it into the 9x13-inch pan.

2. **Bake the Cake:**
   - Bake in the preheated oven for 25-30 minutes, or until a toothpick inserted into the center of the cakes comes out clean.
   - Allow the cakes to cool in the pans for 10 minutes before transferring them to a wire rack to cool completely.

3. **Prepare the Coconut Frosting:**
   - In a large bowl, beat the softened butter until creamy.
   - Gradually add the powdered sugar, beating well after each addition.
   - Mix in the coconut cream and vanilla extract until smooth and fluffy.

4. **Frost the Cake:**
   - Once the cakes are completely cooled, spread a layer of frosting on top of one cake layer (if using two layers) or over the entire surface if using a 9x13-inch pan.
   - Place the second cake layer on top (if using two layers) and frost the top and sides of the cake.
   - Garnish with toasted shredded coconut or fresh coconut flakes, if desired.

5. **Serve:**
   - Slice and serve. The cake can be stored in an airtight container at room temperature for up to 3 days or refrigerated for up to a week.

Tips

- **Coconut Milk:** For the best flavor and texture, use full-fat coconut milk or coconut cream. Light coconut milk can also be used but may result in a less rich cake.
- **Shredded Coconut:** Sweetened shredded coconut adds a touch of extra sweetness, but unsweetened can be used if you prefer less sugar.
- **Toasting Coconut:** Toasting the shredded coconut adds extra flavor and texture. Simply place it in a dry skillet over medium heat, stirring frequently, until golden brown.

This Mexican Coconut Cake is sure to be a hit with its moist texture and rich coconut flavor. Enjoy it as a special treat or for celebrating any occasion!

Flan de Coco (Coconut Flan)

Ingredients

For the Caramel:

- **1 cup granulated sugar**

For the Flan:

- **1 can (14 oz) sweetened condensed milk**
- **1 can (13.5 oz) coconut milk** (full-fat for a richer flavor)
- **4 large eggs**
- **1 teaspoon vanilla extract**
- **1/2 cup shredded coconut** (sweetened or unsweetened, as per your preference)

Instructions

1. **Prepare the Caramel:**
   - In a medium saucepan over medium heat, melt the sugar, stirring constantly, until it turns a deep golden brown. Be careful not to burn it.
   - Immediately pour the caramel into the bottom of a 9-inch round cake pan or a flan mold, tilting the pan to evenly coat the bottom. Set aside to cool and harden.
2. **Prepare the Flan Mixture:**
   - Preheat your oven to 350°F (175°C).
   - In a large bowl, whisk together the sweetened condensed milk, coconut milk, eggs, and vanilla extract until well combined.
   - Stir in the shredded coconut.
3. **Bake the Flan:**
   - Pour the flan mixture over the set caramel in the cake pan.
   - Place the cake pan inside a larger baking dish and create a water bath by adding hot water to the larger dish, about halfway up the sides of the flan pan.
   - Bake in the preheated oven for 50-60 minutes, or until the flan is set and a knife inserted into the center comes out clean.
4. **Cool and Unmold:**
   - Allow the flan to cool to room temperature, then refrigerate for at least 4 hours or overnight to chill and set further.
   - To unmold, run a knife around the edges of the pan to loosen the flan. Place a serving plate over the pan and carefully invert it to release the flan onto the plate.
5. **Serve:**
   - Garnish with additional shredded coconut if desired and serve chilled.

Tips

- **Caramel:** Make sure to work quickly with the caramel as it hardens fast. If it hardens before you can pour it, you can reheat it gently to soften it again.
- **Texture:** The flan should have a smooth, creamy texture. If you find any bubbles or imperfections, gently tap the pan or use a toothpick to smooth it out.
- **Serving:** Flan de Coco is best enjoyed chilled and can be topped with fresh fruit or a dollop of whipped cream for added flair.

Flan de Coco is a delicious and elegant dessert that combines the rich creaminess of flan with the tropical taste of coconut, making it a perfect ending to any meal. Enjoy!

Chocolate Mexicano Truffles

Ingredients

For the Truffles:

- **8 oz (225 g) Mexican chocolate** (chopped, or use semi-sweet chocolate as a substitute)
- **1/2 cup heavy cream**
- **2 tablespoons unsalted butter**
- **1/2 teaspoon ground cinnamon**
- **1/4 teaspoon ground chili powder** (adjust to taste)
- **1/2 teaspoon vanilla extract**
- **Pinch of salt**

For Coating:

- **1/2 cup cocoa powder**
- **1/2 cup finely chopped nuts** (such as almonds, pecans, or hazelnuts) (optional)
- **1/2 cup shredded coconut** (optional)
- **1/2 cup powdered sugar** (optional)

Instructions

1. **Prepare the Ganache:**
   - In a small saucepan, heat the heavy cream over medium heat until it just begins to simmer. Do not let it boil.
   - Place the chopped Mexican chocolate in a heatproof bowl. Pour the hot cream over the chocolate and let it sit for 1-2 minutes to soften.
   - Add the butter, ground cinnamon, chili powder, vanilla extract, and a pinch of salt. Stir until the chocolate and butter are fully melted and the mixture is smooth.
   - Let the ganache cool to room temperature, then cover it and refrigerate for about 1-2 hours, or until it's firm enough to handle.
2. **Form the Truffles:**
   - Once the ganache is firm, use a small scoop or spoon to form balls of the chocolate mixture, about 1 inch in diameter.
   - Roll each ball between your palms to smooth out any imperfections.
3. **Coat the Truffles:**
   - Roll the truffles in cocoa powder, finely chopped nuts, shredded coconut, or powdered sugar, depending on your preference. You can use one or a combination of coatings.
   - Place the coated truffles on a parchment-lined tray.
4. **Chill and Serve:**

- Refrigerate the truffles for about 30 minutes to firm up the coating.
- Serve chilled or at room temperature.

Tips

- **Mexican Chocolate:** If you can't find Mexican chocolate, you can use semi-sweet chocolate or dark chocolate. For an authentic flavor, look for chocolate with cinnamon and other spices if available.
- **Spice Levels:** Adjust the amount of chili powder based on your heat preference. You can also experiment with other spices like a pinch of nutmeg or cayenne pepper for different flavor profiles.
- **Texture:** If the ganache is too soft after chilling, you can refrigerate it a bit longer or mix in a small amount of crushed cookies or graham crackers to make it easier to handle.

These Chocolate Mexicano Truffles are perfect for special occasions or as a treat to enjoy with coffee or dessert wine. They offer a delightful combination of creamy chocolate with a hint of spice, showcasing the rich flavors of Mexican cuisine. Enjoy making and indulging in these delicious truffles!

Mexican Wedding Cake Balls

Ingredients

For the Cake Balls:

- 1 1/2 cups all-purpose flour
- 1 cup unsalted butter (softened)
- 1/2 cup powdered sugar
- 1 cup finely chopped nuts (such as pecans or walnuts)
- 1 teaspoon vanilla extract
- 1/4 teaspoon salt

For the Coating:

- 1 cup powdered sugar (for rolling)
- 1/2 cup finely chopped nuts (optional, for additional coating)
- 1/2 teaspoon ground cinnamon (optional)

Instructions

1. **Prepare the Dough:**
    - Preheat your oven to 350°F (175°C). Line a baking sheet with parchment paper.
    - In a medium bowl, cream the softened butter and powdered sugar until light and fluffy.
    - Gradually mix in the flour, salt, and chopped nuts until combined. The dough will be thick and crumbly.
2. **Shape the Balls:**
    - Roll the dough into small balls, about 1 inch in diameter, and place them on the prepared baking sheet. You can use a small cookie scoop to ensure uniform size.
    - Bake in the preheated oven for 12-15 minutes, or until the edges are lightly golden.
3. **Cool and Coat:**
    - Allow the cake balls to cool on the baking sheet for about 5 minutes before transferring them to a wire rack to cool completely.
    - Once cooled, roll each cake ball in powdered sugar to coat. For extra flavor and texture, you can also roll them in finely chopped nuts mixed with a bit of cinnamon if desired.
4. **Serve:**
    - Place the coated cake balls on a serving platter. They can be stored in an airtight container at room temperature for up to a week or refrigerated for longer freshness.

Tips

- **Texture:** If the dough is too crumbly and difficult to roll, add a small amount of melted butter or a few drops of milk until it holds together better.
- **Flavor Variations:** You can add a dash of ground cinnamon or nutmeg to the dough for extra flavor. Additionally, a touch of orange zest or almond extract can add a unique twist.
- **Coating:** Rolling in powdered sugar right after baking can create a snowy effect, making these treats look like they're dusted with snow, which is traditional for wedding cookies.

Mexican Wedding Cake Balls are a delightful treat that brings the classic flavors of Mexican wedding cookies into a fun, bite-sized form. They're perfect for parties, holiday gatherings, or as a sweet snack any time of year. Enjoy!

Guava Paste and Cheese Dessert

Ingredients

- **8 oz guava paste** (also known as "pasta de guayaba," available at Latin grocery stores)
- **8 oz cream cheese** (or other mild cheese like queso blanco or a soft, mild cheese)
- **Fresh mint leaves** (for garnish, optional)
- **Crackers or sliced baguette** (for serving, optional)

Instructions

1. **Prepare the Ingredients:**
   - Slice the guava paste into thin strips or small squares, depending on your preference.
   - Cut the cream cheese into similar-sized pieces to match the guava paste.
2. **Assemble the Dessert:**
   - Arrange the guava paste and cream cheese pieces on a serving platter.
   - You can layer them alternately or create a more decorative arrangement.
3. **Serve:**
   - Garnish with fresh mint leaves if desired for a touch of color and freshness.
   - Serve with crackers or sliced baguette on the side if you want to add a crunchy element.

Tips

- **Cheese Choices:** While cream cheese is a common choice, you can also use other mild cheeses like queso fresco or even a soft goat cheese for a different flavor profile.
- **Guava Paste:** Guava paste can be quite sweet and sticky. If you find it too sticky to cut, lightly oil your knife or use a serrated knife to slice through it more easily.
- **Presentation:** For an elegant touch, you can drizzle a bit of honey over the cheese before adding the guava paste, or serve with a few nuts like almonds or walnuts for added texture.

Guava Paste and Cheese Dessert is a quick and easy way to enjoy the wonderful combination of sweet and savory flavors. It's perfect for entertaining, a simple dessert after a meal, or even as a special treat for yourself. Enjoy!

Pan de Calabaza (Pumpkin Bread)

Ingredients

For the Bread:

- 1 1/2 cups all-purpose flour
- 1 teaspoon baking powder
- 1/2 teaspoon baking soda
- 1/2 teaspoon salt
- 1 teaspoon ground cinnamon
- 1/2 teaspoon ground nutmeg
- 1/2 teaspoon ground cloves (optional)
- 1/2 cup unsalted butter (softened)
- 1 cup granulated sugar
- 2 large eggs
- 1 cup canned pumpkin puree (not pumpkin pie filling)
- 1/4 cup milk
- 1 teaspoon vanilla extract

For Optional Add-Ins:

- 1/2 cup chopped nuts (such as walnuts or pecans)
- 1/2 cup **chocolate chips** or **raisins** (optional)

For the Glaze (Optional):

- 1/2 cup powdered sugar
- 1-2 tablespoons milk
- 1/4 teaspoon vanilla extract

Instructions

1. **Preheat the Oven:**
    - Preheat your oven to 350°F (175°C). Grease and flour a 9x5-inch loaf pan or line it with parchment paper.
2. **Prepare the Dry Ingredients:**
    - In a medium bowl, whisk together the flour, baking powder, baking soda, salt, cinnamon, nutmeg, and cloves (if using).
3. **Cream the Butter and Sugar:**
    - In a large bowl, cream the softened butter and granulated sugar until light and fluffy.
4. **Add the Eggs:**

- Beat in the eggs one at a time, ensuring each egg is fully incorporated before adding the next.
5. **Add Pumpkin and Vanilla:**
    - Mix in the pumpkin puree and vanilla extract until well combined.
6. **Combine Dry and Wet Ingredients:**
    - Gradually add the dry ingredients to the wet ingredients, alternating with the milk. Begin and end with the dry ingredients. Mix until just combined.
7. **Add Optional Ingredients:**
    - Fold in any optional add-ins like chopped nuts, chocolate chips, or raisins.
8. **Pour and Bake:**
    - Pour the batter into the prepared loaf pan and smooth the top with a spatula.
    - Bake in the preheated oven for 60-70 minutes, or until a toothpick inserted into the center of the bread comes out clean.
9. **Cool and Glaze:**
    - Allow the bread to cool in the pan for 10 minutes before transferring it to a wire rack to cool completely.
    - If using the glaze, whisk together the powdered sugar, milk, and vanilla extract until smooth. Drizzle over the cooled bread.

Tips

- **Pumpkin Purée:** Use canned pumpkin purée, not pumpkin pie filling, which contains additional spices and sugar.
- **Texture:** Ensure the pumpkin bread is fully cooled before slicing to avoid it becoming too crumbly.
- **Storage:** Store in an airtight container at room temperature for up to 5 days. You can also freeze slices of the bread for up to 3 months.

Pan de Calabaza is a wonderful, moist bread that captures the essence of autumn with its spices and pumpkin flavor. It's perfect for cozy gatherings or as a comforting treat any time of the year. Enjoy!

Sweet Corn Cake

Ingredients

- **1 cup cornmeal** (fine or medium grind)
- **1 cup all-purpose flour**
- **1 cup granulated sugar**
- **1/2 cup unsalted butter** (softened)
- **1 cup milk**
- **1 cup canned corn kernels** (drained, or use fresh corn for a more intense corn flavor)
- **3 large eggs**
- **1 tablespoon baking powder**
- **1/2 teaspoon salt**
- **1 teaspoon vanilla extract**
- **1/2 teaspoon ground cinnamon** (optional)

Instructions

1. **Preheat the Oven:**
    - Preheat your oven to 350°F (175°C). Grease and flour an 8-inch round cake pan or a 9x9-inch square baking dish.
2. **Prepare the Cornmeal Mixture:**
    - In a medium bowl, whisk together the cornmeal, flour, baking powder, salt, and ground cinnamon (if using).
3. **Cream the Butter and Sugar:**
    - In a large bowl, cream the softened butter and granulated sugar until light and fluffy.
4. **Add Eggs and Vanilla:**
    - Beat in the eggs one at a time, making sure each egg is fully incorporated before adding the next.
    - Mix in the vanilla extract.
5. **Combine Ingredients:**
    - Gradually add the dry ingredients to the butter mixture, alternating with the milk. Begin and end with the dry ingredients. Mix until just combined.
    - Fold in the canned corn kernels (or fresh corn) until evenly distributed.
6. **Pour and Bake:**
    - Pour the batter into the prepared cake pan and smooth the top with a spatula.
    - Bake in the preheated oven for 30-40 minutes, or until a toothpick inserted into the center of the cake comes out clean and the top is golden brown.
7. **Cool and Serve:**
    - Allow the cake to cool in the pan for 10 minutes before transferring it to a wire rack to cool completely.

- Slice and serve. The cake can be enjoyed warm or at room temperature.

Tips

- **Corn Flavor:** For a more intense corn flavor, you can use fresh corn kernels and blend them into a puree before adding them to the batter.
- **Texture:** If you prefer a denser texture, you can use a coarser grind of cornmeal. For a smoother texture, use fine cornmeal.
- **Variations:** You can add ingredients like blueberries, raspberries, or a swirl of caramel for extra flavor. A sprinkle of powdered sugar on top can also add a touch of sweetness.

Sweet Corn Cake is a delightful and comforting treat with a lovely balance of sweetness and the distinct flavor of corn. It's perfect for any occasion and pairs wonderfully with a cup of coffee or tea. Enjoy!

Chocoflan with Kahlúa

Ingredients

For the Caramel:

- 1 cup granulated sugar

For the Flan Layer:

- 1 can (14 oz) sweetened condensed milk
- 1 can (13.5 oz) evaporated milk
- 4 large eggs
- 1/2 cup Kahlúa
- 1 teaspoon vanilla extract

For the Chocolate Cake Layer:

- 1 cup all-purpose flour
- 1 cup granulated sugar
- 1/3 cup unsweetened cocoa powder
- 1 teaspoon baking powder
- 1/2 teaspoon baking soda
- 1/4 teaspoon salt
- 1/2 cup milk
- 1/4 cup vegetable oil
- 1 large egg
- 1/2 teaspoon vanilla extract
- 1/2 cup boiling water

Instructions

1. **Prepare the Caramel:**
   - In a medium saucepan over medium heat, melt the sugar, stirring constantly until it turns a deep golden brown. Be careful not to burn it.
   - Immediately pour the caramel into the bottom of a 9-inch round cake pan or a flan mold, tilting the pan to evenly coat the bottom. Set aside to cool and harden.
2. **Prepare the Flan Mixture:**
   - In a large bowl, whisk together the sweetened condensed milk, evaporated milk, eggs, Kahlúa, and vanilla extract until well combined.
3. **Prepare the Chocolate Cake Batter:**
   - In a medium bowl, sift together the flour, sugar, cocoa powder, baking powder, baking soda, and salt.
   - In another bowl, whisk together the milk, vegetable oil, egg, and vanilla extract.
   - Gradually add the wet ingredients to the dry ingredients, mixing until just combined.
   - Stir in the boiling water until the batter is smooth (the batter will be thin).

4. **Assemble the Cake:**
   - Pour the flan mixture over the set caramel in the cake pan.
   - Carefully pour the chocolate cake batter on top of the flan mixture. It will seem like the layers are mixing, but they will separate during baking.
5. **Bake the Cake:**
   - Place the cake pan inside a larger baking dish and add hot water to the larger dish, about halfway up the sides of the cake pan to create a water bath.
   - Bake in the preheated oven for 60-70 minutes, or until a toothpick inserted into the center of the cake comes out clean.
6. **Cool and Unmold:**
   - Allow the cake to cool in the pan for about 15 minutes. Then, run a knife around the edges to loosen it.
   - Invert the cake onto a serving plate. The caramel should flow over the cake, and the layers will be in their proper places with the flan on top and the chocolate cake on the bottom.
7. **Serve:**
   - Chill the Chocoflan in the refrigerator for at least 4 hours or overnight to set completely.
   - Serve chilled. Optionally, garnish with whipped cream or fresh berries.

Tips

- **Caramel:** Be cautious when making caramel as it can burn quickly. If it hardens before you pour it, gently reheat it to soften.
- **Layering:** The magic of Chocoflan is that the flan layer ends up on top, but make sure not to mix the layers when adding them to the pan.
- **Kahlúa:** Adjust the amount of Kahlúa based on your preference for the coffee flavor. You can also substitute it with another coffee liqueur if desired.

Chocoflan with Kahlúa is an elegant and impressive dessert that blends the best of both worlds—rich chocolate and smooth flan with a hint of coffee liqueur. It's perfect for special occasions or as a delightful treat for any time. Enjoy!

Dulce de Leche Flan

Ingredients

For the Caramel:

- 1 cup granulated sugar

For the Flan:

- 1 can (14 oz) sweetened condensed milk
- 1 can (12 oz) evaporated milk
- 1/2 cup dulce de leche
- 4 large eggs
- 1 teaspoon vanilla extract
- Pinch of salt

Instructions

1. **Prepare the Caramel:**
    - In a medium saucepan over medium heat, melt the sugar, stirring constantly, until it turns a deep golden brown. Be careful not to burn it.
    - Immediately pour the caramel into the bottom of a 9-inch round cake pan or a flan mold, tilting the pan to evenly coat the bottom. Set aside to cool and harden.
2. **Prepare the Flan Mixture:**
    - In a large bowl, whisk together the sweetened condensed milk, evaporated milk, and dulce de leche until smooth and well combined.
    - Beat in the eggs one at a time, making sure each egg is fully incorporated before adding the next.
    - Mix in the vanilla extract and a pinch of salt.
3. **Bake the Flan:**
    - Preheat your oven to 350°F (175°C).
    - Pour the flan mixture over the cooled caramel in the cake pan.
    - Place the cake pan inside a larger baking dish and add hot water to the larger dish, about halfway up the sides of the flan pan to create a water bath.
    - Bake in the preheated oven for 50-60 minutes, or until the flan is set and a knife inserted into the center comes out clean.
4. **Cool and Unmold:**
    - Allow the flan to cool to room temperature, then refrigerate for at least 4 hours or overnight to chill and set further.
    - To unmold, run a knife around the edges of the pan to loosen the flan. Place a serving plate over the pan and carefully invert it to release the flan onto the plate.
5. **Serve:**

- Garnish with additional caramel sauce, if desired, or serve with a dollop of whipped cream.

Tips

- **Caramel:** Make sure to work quickly with the caramel as it hardens fast. If it hardens before you can pour it, gently reheat it to soften it again.
- **Texture:** The flan should have a smooth, creamy texture. If you find any bubbles or imperfections, gently tap the pan or use a toothpick to smooth it out.
- **Serving:** Flan is best enjoyed chilled and can be topped with fresh fruit or a sprinkle of sea salt for added flavor.

Dulce de Leche Flan is a rich and luxurious dessert that brings together the creamy texture of flan with the deep, caramel flavor of dulce de leche. It's perfect for special occasions or as a decadent treat anytime. Enjoy!

Mango with Tajín

Ingredients

- **2 ripe mangoes** (peeled, pitted, and sliced)
- **Tajín seasoning** (to taste)
- **Lime wedges** (optional, for extra tang)
- **Chili powder or hot sauce** (optional, for added spice)

Instructions

1. **Prepare the Mango:**
   - Peel and slice the mangoes. To do this, cut the mangoes on either side of the pit, then slice the flesh into thin strips or bite-sized pieces. You can also scoop the flesh out of the skin using a spoon if you prefer.
2. **Season the Mango:**
   - Arrange the mango slices on a serving plate or in a bowl.
   - Sprinkle Tajín seasoning generously over the mango slices. Adjust the amount based on your preference for spiciness and tanginess.
3. **Add Extra Flavor (Optional):**
   - For an extra zing, squeeze fresh lime juice over the mango slices. This adds a refreshing citrusy note that complements the Tajín.
   - If you like it spicier, you can sprinkle a bit of chili powder or drizzle some hot sauce over the mango slices.
4. **Serve:**
   - Serve immediately as a fresh snack or light dessert. It can also be enjoyed as part of a larger spread or as a refreshing side dish.

Tips

- **Mango Ripeness:** Choose ripe mangoes that yield slightly to gentle pressure. They should be sweet and juicy. Unripe mangoes can be too firm and sour.
- **Tajín:** Tajín is a blend of chili peppers, lime, and salt. If you don't have Tajín, you can substitute with a mix of chili powder, salt, and a little lime zest.
- **Adjusting Spice Levels:** If you're not sure how spicy you want it, start with a light sprinkle of Tajín and add more to taste.

Mango with Tajín is a vibrant and tasty treat that perfectly balances sweet, spicy, and tangy flavors. It's a great way to enjoy fresh fruit with a kick of flavor. Enjoy!

Piñata Cupcakes

Ingredients

For the Cupcakes:

- 1 1/2 cups all-purpose flour
- 1 1/2 teaspoons baking powder
- 1/4 teaspoon salt
- **1/2 cup unsalted butter** (softened)
- **1 cup granulated sugar**
- **2 large eggs**
- **1 teaspoon vanilla extract**
- **1/2 cup milk**

For the Filling:

- **1/2 cup mini chocolate chips** (or any small candy, sprinkles, or colored candy pieces)

For the Frosting:

- **1/2 cup unsalted butter** (softened)
- **1 1/2 cups powdered sugar**
- **1-2 tablespoons milk**
- **1 teaspoon vanilla extract**
- **Food coloring** (optional, for decorating)

For Decorating:

- **Sprinkles** (or additional candies for topping)
- **Edible glitter** (optional)

Instructions

1. **Preheat the Oven:**
   - Preheat your oven to 350°F (175°C). Line a muffin tin with paper cupcake liners.
2. **Make the Cupcake Batter:**
   - In a medium bowl, whisk together the flour, baking powder, and salt.
   - In a large bowl, cream the softened butter and granulated sugar until light and fluffy.
   - Beat in the eggs one at a time, ensuring each egg is fully incorporated before adding the next.
   - Mix in the vanilla extract.

- Gradually add the dry ingredients to the butter mixture, alternating with the milk. Begin and end with the dry ingredients. Mix until just combined.
3. **Bake the Cupcakes:**
   - Fill each cupcake liner about 2/3 full with the batter.
   - Bake in the preheated oven for 18-22 minutes, or until a toothpick inserted into the center of a cupcake comes out clean.
   - Allow the cupcakes to cool in the pan for 5 minutes before transferring them to a wire rack to cool completely.
4. **Prepare the Filling:**
   - Once the cupcakes are completely cooled, use a small knife or cupcake corer to carefully remove a small portion from the center of each cupcake, creating a cavity.
   - Fill the cavity with mini chocolate chips, candy pieces, or sprinkles.
5. **Frost the Cupcakes:**
   - In a large bowl, beat the softened butter until creamy.
   - Gradually add the powdered sugar, beating well after each addition.
   - Mix in the vanilla extract and enough milk to achieve your desired frosting consistency.
   - If using, add food coloring to tint the frosting.
   - Frost the cooled cupcakes with the prepared frosting using a spatula or piping bag.
6. **Decorate:**
   - Top the frosted cupcakes with sprinkles, additional candies, or edible glitter for a festive touch.

Tips

- **Filling:** Ensure that the cavity in the cupcakes is large enough to hold a good amount of filling but not so large that the cupcake structure becomes unstable.
- **Frosting Consistency:** If the frosting is too thick, add a bit more milk, a teaspoon at a time. If it's too thin, add a little more powdered sugar.
- **Serving:** For the best results, fill and frost the cupcakes just before serving to ensure the filling remains fresh and the frosting stays crisp.

Piñata Cupcakes are not only a treat for the taste buds but also a delightful surprise that adds an element of fun to any occasion. Enjoy making and sharing these festive cupcakes!

Mexican Hot Chocolate Cupcakes

Ingredients

For the Cupcakes:

- 1 1/2 cups all-purpose flour
- 1 cup granulated sugar
- 1/2 cup unsweetened cocoa powder
- 1 1/2 teaspoons baking powder
- 1/2 teaspoon baking soda
- 1/2 teaspoon salt
- 1 teaspoon ground cinnamon
- 1/4 teaspoon ground nutmeg (optional)
- 1/2 cup unsalted butter (softened)
- 2 large eggs
- 1 teaspoon vanilla extract
- 1/2 cup milk
- 1/2 cup boiling water
- 1/4 cup finely chopped dark chocolate (optional, for extra richness)

For the Frosting:

- 1/2 cup unsalted butter (softened)
- 1 1/2 cups powdered sugar
- 1/4 cup unsweetened cocoa powder
- 1-2 tablespoons milk
- 1 teaspoon vanilla extract
- 1/2 teaspoon ground cinnamon
- **A pinch of ground cayenne pepper** (optional, for a hint of spice)

For Garnishing:

- **A sprinkle of ground cinnamon or cocoa powder**
- **Whipped cream** (optional)

Instructions

1. **Preheat the Oven:**
    - Preheat your oven to 350°F (175°C). Line a muffin tin with paper cupcake liners.
2. **Make the Cupcake Batter:**
    - In a medium bowl, whisk together the flour, sugar, cocoa powder, baking powder, baking soda, salt, cinnamon, and nutmeg (if using).

- In a large bowl, cream the softened butter until light and fluffy.
- Beat in the eggs one at a time, mixing well after each addition. Add the vanilla extract.
- Gradually add the dry ingredients to the butter mixture, alternating with the milk. Begin and end with the dry ingredients. Mix until just combined.
- Stir in the boiling water. The batter will be thin, but this is normal.
- If using, fold in the finely chopped dark chocolate for extra richness.

3. **Bake the Cupcakes:**
    - Fill each cupcake liner about 2/3 full with batter.
    - Bake in the preheated oven for 18-22 minutes, or until a toothpick inserted into the center of a cupcake comes out clean.
    - Allow the cupcakes to cool in the pan for 5 minutes before transferring them to a wire rack to cool completely.

4. **Prepare the Frosting:**
    - In a large bowl, beat the softened butter until creamy.
    - Gradually add the powdered sugar and cocoa powder, mixing well after each addition.
    - Mix in the vanilla extract, ground cinnamon, and a pinch of cayenne pepper (if using). Add enough milk to achieve your desired frosting consistency.

5. **Frost the Cupcakes:**
    - Once the cupcakes are completely cooled, frost them with the prepared frosting using a spatula or a piping bag.
    - Garnish with a sprinkle of ground cinnamon or cocoa powder, and optionally, top with a dollop of whipped cream.

Tips

- **Texture:** For a lighter cupcake, ensure the butter is creamed well and avoid overmixing the batter.
- **Spice Level:** Adjust the amount of cinnamon and cayenne pepper to your taste. The cayenne is optional but adds a subtle kick that enhances the flavor.
- **Storage:** Store frosted cupcakes in an airtight container at room temperature for up to 3 days or refrigerate for up to a week.

Mexican Hot Chocolate Cupcakes offer a delightful blend of flavors reminiscent of the classic drink, with a touch of spice and rich chocolate. They're a perfect treat for cooler weather or any time you want to indulge in a bit of comfort. Enjoy!

Mexican Rice Pudding with Cinnamon

Ingredients

- **1 cup long-grain white rice** (rinsed)
- **2 cups water**
- **1 cinnamon stick**
- **1 can (12 oz) evaporated milk**
- **1 can (14 oz) sweetened condensed milk**
- **2 cups whole milk**
- **1/2 cup raisins** (optional)
- **1/4 teaspoon ground cinnamon** (for garnish)
- **1/4 teaspoon vanilla extract** (optional)

Instructions

1. **Cook the Rice:**
   - In a medium saucepan, combine the rinsed rice and water. Add the cinnamon stick.
   - Bring to a boil over medium-high heat, then reduce the heat to low and simmer, covered, for about 15-20 minutes, or until the rice is tender and most of the water is absorbed.
2. **Add the Milks:**
   - Once the rice is cooked, add the evaporated milk, sweetened condensed milk, and whole milk to the saucepan. Stir to combine.
   - Increase the heat to medium and cook, stirring frequently, until the mixture begins to thicken, about 10-15 minutes. Be careful not to let it boil over.
3. **Add Raisins (Optional):**
   - If using raisins, stir them in and cook for an additional 5 minutes, or until the pudding has thickened to your desired consistency.
4. **Finish and Serve:**
   - Remove the cinnamon stick from the pudding.
   - Stir in the vanilla extract if using.
   - Spoon the pudding into serving dishes. Sprinkle with ground cinnamon on top.
5. **Chill (Optional):**
   - You can serve the rice pudding warm, or let it cool to room temperature and refrigerate for a few hours to serve chilled.

Tips

- **Texture:** The rice pudding will continue to thicken as it cools. If it becomes too thick, you can stir in a little additional milk to reach your desired consistency.

- **Flavor Variations:** For extra flavor, you can add a pinch of nutmeg or cloves along with the cinnamon. Some people also like to add a splash of orange zest or a small amount of lemon zest.
- **Serving:** Rice pudding can be served on its own or with fresh fruit, nuts, or a drizzle of honey for added sweetness.

Mexican Rice Pudding with Cinnamon is a deliciously comforting dessert that's perfect for any time of year. Whether you enjoy it warm or cold, this classic treat is sure to be a hit with family and friends. Enjoy!

Pecan Pralines with Mexican Chocolate

Ingredients

- **1 cup pecan halves**
- **1 cup granulated sugar**
- **1/2 cup light brown sugar** (packed)
- **1/2 cup unsalted butter** (cubed)
- **1/2 cup heavy cream**
- **1/2 teaspoon vanilla extract**
- **1/4 teaspoon ground cinnamon**
- **1/4 teaspoon ground cayenne pepper** (optional, for a hint of spice)
- **2 ounces Mexican chocolate** (finely chopped) (Mexican chocolate is typically sweet and flavored with cinnamon)
- **Pinch of salt**

Instructions

1. **Prepare the Pecans:**
    - Toast the pecan halves in a dry skillet over medium heat for about 3-5 minutes, stirring frequently, until they are fragrant and lightly browned. Be careful not to burn them. Set aside.
2. **Cook the Praline Mixture:**
    - In a medium saucepan over medium heat, combine the granulated sugar, brown sugar, butter, and heavy cream.
    - Stir continuously until the mixture comes to a boil.
    - Reduce the heat to medium-low and continue to cook, stirring frequently, for about 8-10 minutes, or until the mixture reaches the soft-ball stage (235-240°F or 113-115°C on a candy thermometer).
3. **Add Flavorings and Pecans:**
    - Remove the saucepan from the heat and stir in the vanilla extract, ground cinnamon, cayenne pepper (if using), and a pinch of salt.
    - Fold in the finely chopped Mexican chocolate until it is completely melted and incorporated.
    - Stir in the toasted pecans.
4. **Shape the Pralines:**
    - Drop spoonfuls of the praline mixture onto a parchment-lined baking sheet, forming small clusters or rounds.
    - Let the pralines cool and set at room temperature. They will firm up as they cool.
5. **Store and Serve:**
    - Once completely cooled and set, store the pecan pralines in an airtight container at room temperature for up to a week.

Tips

- **Candy Thermometer:** Using a candy thermometer is crucial for getting the right consistency. If you don't have one, test the mixture by dropping a small amount into a glass of cold water. It should form a soft ball that you can easily shape with your fingers.
- **Mexican Chocolate:** Mexican chocolate has a unique flavor due to the added cinnamon and sometimes vanilla. If you can't find it, you can use a good quality dark chocolate and add a pinch of cinnamon.
- **Texture:** If the praline mixture seems too soft after cooling, it may need a bit more cooking next time. Conversely, if it becomes too hard, try cooking it for a shorter time.

Pecan Pralines with Mexican Chocolate are a decadent treat that offers a delightful blend of nutty, chocolatey, and spicy flavors. They make a wonderful gift or a special addition to any dessert table. Enjoy!

Mexican Cinnamon Rolls

Ingredients

For the Dough:

- **1 cup warm milk** (110°F or 45°C)
- **1/4 cup granulated sugar**
- **2 1/4 teaspoons active dry yeast** (1 packet)
- **1/2 cup unsalted butter** (softened)
- **1 large egg**
- **1/2 teaspoon vanilla extract**
- **4 cups all-purpose flour**
- **1/2 teaspoon salt**

For the Filling:

- **1/2 cup unsalted butter** (softened)
- **1 cup brown sugar** (packed)
- **2 tablespoons ground cinnamon**
- **1/4 cup finely chopped Mexican chocolate** (optional, for a hint of extra flavor)

For the Glaze:

- **1 cup powdered sugar**
- **2 tablespoons milk**
- **1/2 teaspoon vanilla extract**
- **1/4 teaspoon ground cinnamon**

Instructions

1. **Prepare the Dough:**
   - In a small bowl, combine the warm milk and granulated sugar. Sprinkle the yeast over the top and let it sit for about 5 minutes, or until foamy.
   - In a large mixing bowl, combine the flour and salt. Make a well in the center and add the yeast mixture, softened butter, egg, and vanilla extract.
   - Mix until a dough forms, then turn it out onto a lightly floured surface and knead for about 5-7 minutes, or until smooth and elastic.
   - Place the dough in a lightly greased bowl, cover it with a clean cloth or plastic wrap, and let it rise in a warm place for about 1-1.5 hours, or until doubled in size.
2. **Prepare the Filling:**
   - In a medium bowl, mix together the softened butter, brown sugar, and ground cinnamon until well combined. If using Mexican chocolate, stir it in as well.

3. **Assemble the Rolls:**
    - Once the dough has risen, punch it down and turn it out onto a lightly floured surface. Roll it out into a rectangle about 16x12 inches.
    - Spread the cinnamon-sugar mixture evenly over the dough, leaving a small border around the edges.
    - Starting from one long side, roll the dough tightly into a log. Pinch the seams to seal.
    - Cut the log into 12 even slices and place them in a greased 9x13-inch baking dish or on a parchment-lined baking sheet.
4. **Second Rise:**
    - Cover the rolls loosely with plastic wrap or a clean cloth and let them rise for another 30 minutes, or until puffed.
5. **Bake the Rolls:**
    - Preheat your oven to 350°F (175°C).
    - Bake the rolls in the preheated oven for 20-25 minutes, or until golden brown and cooked through.
6. **Prepare the Glaze:**
    - While the rolls are baking, mix together the powdered sugar, milk, vanilla extract, and ground cinnamon in a small bowl until smooth.
    - If the glaze is too thick, add a little more milk, one teaspoon at a time, until it reaches your desired consistency.
7. **Glaze and Serve:**
    - Once the rolls are baked and still warm, drizzle the glaze over them.
    - Serve warm or at room temperature.

Tips

- **Dough Consistency:** If the dough feels too sticky, add a little more flour, a tablespoon at a time, until it's manageable.
- **Chocolate Addition:** Mexican chocolate adds a nice touch, but if you prefer a more traditional roll, you can omit it.
- **Storage:** Cinnamon rolls are best enjoyed fresh, but you can store them in an airtight container at room temperature for up to 3 days. They can also be frozen for up to 3 months; just reheat before serving.

Mexican Cinnamon Rolls offer a delightful twist on a classic treat, with the rich, warm flavors of cinnamon and a touch of Mexican chocolate. They're perfect for starting the day on a sweet note or enjoying as a special dessert. Enjoy!

Churro Cheesecake

Ingredients

For the Crust:

- **1 1/2 cups graham cracker crumbs**
- **1/4 cup granulated sugar**
- **1/2 cup unsalted butter** (melted)

For the Churro Filling:

- **2 cups cream cheese** (softened)
- **1 cup sour cream**
- **1 cup granulated sugar**
- **1 teaspoon vanilla extract**
- **3 large eggs**
- **1/4 cup all-purpose flour**
- **1 teaspoon ground cinnamon**
- **1/2 teaspoon salt**

For the Churro Topping:

- **1/4 cup granulated sugar**
- **1 teaspoon ground cinnamon**
- **1/2 cup mini churros** (store-bought or homemade, optional)

For the Caramel Sauce (Optional):

- **1/2 cup caramel sauce** (store-bought or homemade)

Instructions

1. **Prepare the Crust:**
    - Preheat your oven to 325°F (163°C).
    - In a medium bowl, combine the graham cracker crumbs, granulated sugar, and melted butter. Mix until the crumbs are evenly coated.
    - Press the mixture firmly into the bottom of a 9-inch springform pan to form an even crust.
    - Bake the crust in the preheated oven for 8-10 minutes. Remove and let it cool while you prepare the filling.
2. **Prepare the Churro Filling:**
    - In a large mixing bowl, beat the softened cream cheese until smooth and creamy.
    - Add the sour cream, granulated sugar, and vanilla extract. Beat until well combined.

- Add the eggs one at a time, mixing well after each addition.
- Mix in the flour, ground cinnamon, and salt until just combined.
- Pour the filling over the pre-baked crust and smooth the top with a spatula.

3. **Bake the Cheesecake:**
    - Place the springform pan on a baking sheet to catch any drips.
    - Bake in the preheated oven for 55-65 minutes, or until the center is set and the edges are lightly browned.
    - Turn off the oven and crack the oven door slightly. Let the cheesecake cool in the oven for 1 hour to prevent cracking.
    - Remove the cheesecake from the oven and let it cool to room temperature. Then refrigerate for at least 4 hours or overnight to fully set.

4. **Prepare the Churro Topping:**
    - In a small bowl, mix together the granulated sugar and ground cinnamon.
    - Once the cheesecake is fully chilled, remove it from the springform pan and sprinkle the cinnamon sugar mixture evenly over the top.
    - Garnish with mini churros if desired.

5. **Serve:**
    - Drizzle caramel sauce over the cheesecake slices if you like extra sweetness.
    - Serve chilled and enjoy!

Tips

- **Cheesecake Consistency:** Make sure the cream cheese is softened to avoid lumps in your filling. Also, mixing on low speed helps prevent air bubbles.
- **Prevent Cracking:** Avoid overmixing the batter and ensure the cheesecake is fully cooled before refrigerating to minimize cracking.
- **Mini Churros:** If using mini churros, you can find them at some grocery stores or make your own. They add a fun and crunchy texture.

Churro Cheesecake blends the creamy, smooth texture of cheesecake with the sweet and spicy flavors of churros, creating a dessert that's both indulgent and unique. Perfect for special occasions or as a standout treat for any gathering! Enjoy!

Sweet Potato Flan

Ingredients

For the Caramel:

- **1 cup granulated sugar**
- **1/4 cup water**

For the Flan:

- **1 cup mashed sweet potato** (about 1 medium sweet potato, cooked and mashed)
- **1 can (12 oz) evaporated milk**
- **1 can (14 oz) sweetened condensed milk**
- **4 large eggs**
- **1 teaspoon vanilla extract**
- **1/2 teaspoon ground cinnamon**
- **1/4 teaspoon ground nutmeg**
- **Pinch of salt**

Instructions

1. **Prepare the Caramel:**
   - In a medium saucepan over medium heat, combine the granulated sugar and water.
   - Cook, without stirring, until the sugar dissolves and turns a deep amber color, about 8-10 minutes. Swirl the pan gently if needed to ensure even coloring.
   - Carefully pour the hot caramel into the bottom of a 9-inch round baking dish or flan mold, tilting the dish to evenly coat the bottom. Allow it to cool and harden while you prepare the flan mixture.
2. **Prepare the Flan Mixture:**
   - Preheat your oven to 350°F (175°C).
   - In a large mixing bowl, whisk together the mashed sweet potato, evaporated milk, sweetened condensed milk, eggs, vanilla extract, ground cinnamon, ground nutmeg, and a pinch of salt until well combined and smooth.
   - Strain the mixture through a fine mesh sieve to ensure a silky texture.
3. **Bake the Flan:**
   - Pour the sweet potato flan mixture over the set caramel in the baking dish.
   - Place the baking dish in a larger baking pan and add hot water to the larger pan, creating a water bath (about halfway up the sides of the flan dish).
   - Bake in the preheated oven for 60-70 minutes, or until the flan is set and a knife inserted into the center comes out clean.
4. **Cool and Unmold:**
   - Remove the flan from the oven and the water bath. Allow it to cool to room temperature.
   - Cover and refrigerate for at least 4 hours or overnight to fully set.
5. **Serve:**

- To unmold, run a knife around the edges of the flan to loosen it. Place a serving plate over the top of the flan dish and invert it to release the flan onto the plate.
- The caramel will flow over the top of the flan, creating a delicious sauce.

Tips

- **Sweet Potato Preparation:** Bake or steam the sweet potato until tender, then peel and mash it well. Ensure there are no lumps for a smooth flan texture.
- **Caramel Safety:** Be cautious when working with hot caramel, as it can cause burns. Let it cool completely before handling.
- **Water Bath:** The water bath helps cook the flan evenly and prevents it from cracking. Make sure the water is hot when adding it to the pan.

Sweet Potato Flan is a creamy and indulgent dessert that offers a unique and flavorful twist on the classic flan. Its rich texture and caramelized sweetness make it a perfect end to any meal. Enjoy!

Horchata Ice Cream

Ingredients

- **1 cup rice** (short-grain or medium-grain)
- **2 cups water**
- **2 cups whole milk**
- **1 cup heavy cream**
- **3/4 cup granulated sugar**
- **1/4 cup light brown sugar** (packed)
- **1 tablespoon vanilla extract**
- **1 teaspoon ground cinnamon**
- **Pinch of salt**

Instructions

1. **Prepare the Rice Mixture:**
   - Rinse the rice under cold water until the water runs clear.
   - In a medium saucepan, combine the rinsed rice and 2 cups of water. Bring to a boil, then reduce the heat to low and simmer, covered, for about 15-20 minutes, or until the rice is tender and the water is absorbed.
   - Let the rice cool slightly, then transfer it to a blender or food processor. Blend with 1 cup of milk until smooth.
2. **Combine the Mixture:**
   - In a large bowl, whisk together the rice mixture, remaining 1 cup of milk, heavy cream, granulated sugar, light brown sugar, vanilla extract, ground cinnamon, and a pinch of salt until the sugars are completely dissolved.
3. **Chill the Mixture:**
   - Cover the mixture and refrigerate it for at least 2 hours, or until it is thoroughly chilled.
4. **Churn the Ice Cream:**
   - Pour the chilled mixture into an ice cream maker and churn according to the manufacturer's instructions. This typically takes about 20-25 minutes, or until the ice cream reaches a soft-serve consistency.
5. **Freeze to Firm Up:**
   - Transfer the churned ice cream to an airtight container and freeze for an additional 2-4 hours, or until firm.
6. **Serve:**
   - Scoop and serve the horchata ice cream. Optionally, you can sprinkle a little extra ground cinnamon on top for added flavor.

Tips

- **Rice Type:** Short-grain or medium-grain rice works best because it blends into a smooth, creamy texture. Long-grain rice may not blend as smoothly.

- **Blending:** Ensure the rice is well-blended for a smooth consistency in the ice cream. You might need to blend in batches depending on your blender's capacity.
- **Ice Cream Maker:** If you don't have an ice cream maker, you can place the mixture in a freezer-safe container and stir every 30 minutes to break up ice crystals until it reaches the desired consistency.

Horchata Ice Cream is a unique and delicious way to enjoy the flavors of traditional horchata in a frozen format. It's perfect for hot days or as a special treat for any occasion. Enjoy!

Mexican Hot Chocolate Cake

Ingredients

For the Cake:

- 1 3/4 cups all-purpose flour
- 1 1/2 cups granulated sugar
- 3/4 cup unsweetened cocoa powder
- 1 1/2 teaspoons baking powder
- 1 1/2 teaspoons baking soda
- 1/2 teaspoon salt
- 1 teaspoon ground cinnamon
- 1/4 teaspoon ground cayenne pepper (optional, for a subtle kick)
- 1 cup whole milk
- 1/2 cup vegetable oil
- 2 large eggs
- 2 teaspoons vanilla extract
- 1 cup boiling water
- 1/2 cup finely chopped Mexican chocolate (optional, for extra richness)

For the Frosting:

- 1 cup unsalted butter (softened)
- 3 cups powdered sugar
- 1/2 cup unsweetened cocoa powder
- 1/4 cup whole milk (more if needed)
- 1 teaspoon vanilla extract
- 1/2 teaspoon ground cinnamon

For Garnishing (Optional):

- Whipped cream
- Shaved chocolate or cocoa powder

Instructions

1. **Prepare the Cake Batter:**
   - Preheat your oven to 350°F (175°C). Grease and flour two 9-inch round cake pans or line them with parchment paper.
   - In a large mixing bowl, whisk together the flour, granulated sugar, cocoa powder, baking powder, baking soda, salt, ground cinnamon, and cayenne pepper (if using).
   - Add the milk, vegetable oil, eggs, and vanilla extract. Mix until well combined.

- Gradually add the boiling water, mixing on low speed until smooth. The batter will be thin, but this is normal.
- If using, fold in the finely chopped Mexican chocolate.

2. **Bake the Cake:**
   - Divide the batter evenly between the prepared cake pans.
   - Bake in the preheated oven for 25-30 minutes, or until a toothpick inserted into the center comes out clean.
   - Allow the cakes to cool in the pans for 10 minutes, then turn them out onto wire racks to cool completely.

3. **Prepare the Frosting:**
   - In a large bowl, beat the softened butter until creamy.
   - Gradually add the powdered sugar and cocoa powder, mixing well after each addition.
   - Add the milk, vanilla extract, and ground cinnamon. Beat until the frosting is smooth and spreadable. Adjust the milk if needed to achieve your desired consistency.

4. **Assemble and Frost the Cake:**
   - Place one cake layer on a serving plate or cake stand.
   - Spread a layer of frosting on top of the first layer.
   - Place the second cake layer on top and frost the top and sides of the cake.

5. **Garnish and Serve:**
   - Garnish with whipped cream and shaved chocolate or a dusting of cocoa powder if desired.
   - Serve and enjoy!

Tips

- **Mexican Chocolate:** For a more intense chocolate flavor, use finely chopped Mexican chocolate or add chocolate chips to the batter.
- **Texture:** If the cake layers domed in the center, level them with a knife before frosting for a smoother appearance.
- **Cayenne Pepper:** The cayenne pepper adds a subtle heat that complements the chocolate. Adjust the amount based on your preference.

Mexican Hot Chocolate Cake is a delightful and flavorful dessert that combines the comforting spices of Mexican hot chocolate with the indulgence of a rich chocolate cake. It's perfect for special occasions or a treat to enjoy anytime. Enjoy!

Vanilla Mexican Flan

Ingredients

For the Caramel:

- 1 cup granulated sugar
- 1/4 cup water

For the Flan:

- 1 can (12 oz) evaporated milk
- 1 can (14 oz) sweetened condensed milk
- 4 large eggs
- 1 tablespoon vanilla extract
- 1/4 teaspoon salt

Instructions

1. **Prepare the Caramel:**
   - In a medium saucepan over medium heat, combine the granulated sugar and water.
   - Cook, without stirring, until the sugar dissolves and turns a deep amber color, about 8-10 minutes. Swirl the pan gently if needed to ensure even coloring.
   - Carefully pour the hot caramel into the bottom of a 9-inch round baking dish or flan mold, tilting the dish to evenly coat the bottom. Allow it to cool and harden while you prepare the flan mixture.
2. **Prepare the Flan Mixture:**
   - Preheat your oven to 350°F (175°C).
   - In a large mixing bowl, whisk together the evaporated milk, sweetened condensed milk, eggs, vanilla extract, and salt until well combined and smooth.
   - Strain the mixture through a fine mesh sieve into another bowl to ensure a silky texture and to remove any lumps.
3. **Bake the Flan:**
   - Pour the flan mixture over the set caramel in the baking dish.
   - Place the baking dish in a larger baking pan and add hot water to the larger pan, creating a water bath (about halfway up the sides of the flan dish).
   - Bake in the preheated oven for 50-60 minutes, or until the flan is set and a knife inserted into the center comes out clean.
4. **Cool and Unmold:**
   - Remove the flan from the oven and the water bath. Allow it to cool to room temperature.
   - Cover and refrigerate for at least 4 hours or overnight to fully set.
5. **Serve:**

- To unmold, run a knife around the edges of the flan to loosen it. Place a serving plate over the top of the flan dish and invert it to release the flan onto the plate.
- The caramel will flow over the top of the flan, creating a delicious sauce.

Tips

- **Caramel Safety:** Be cautious when working with hot caramel, as it can cause burns. Let it cool completely before handling.
- **Smooth Texture:** Straining the flan mixture helps achieve a smooth, silky texture. Make sure to strain it even if the mixture appears smooth.
- **Water Bath:** The water bath helps cook the flan evenly and prevents it from cracking. Make sure the water is hot when adding it to the pan.

Vanilla Mexican Flan is a timeless dessert that combines the richness of vanilla with a creamy custard and caramelized sugar. It's a perfect finish to any meal and is sure to impress with its elegance and flavor. Enjoy!

Plantain Fritters

Ingredients

- **2 ripe plantains** (yellow with a few black spots, not too soft)
- **1/4 cup all-purpose flour**
- **2 tablespoons sugar** (adjust based on your preference for sweetness, or omit for savory fritters)
- **1/4 teaspoon ground cinnamon** (optional, for a sweet version)
- **1/4 teaspoon salt**
- **1 large egg**
- **1/2 teaspoon vanilla extract** (optional, for a sweet version)
- **1/2 teaspoon baking powder**
- **Oil for frying** (vegetable, canola, or coconut oil)

Instructions

1. **Prepare the Plantains:**
    - Peel the plantains and cut them into chunks.
    - In a blender or food processor, blend the plantain chunks until smooth. You can also mash them with a fork if you prefer a chunkier texture.
2. **Mix the Batter:**
    - In a large mixing bowl, combine the plantain puree, flour, sugar, ground cinnamon (if using), salt, egg, vanilla extract (if using), and baking powder. Mix until well combined. The batter should be thick but pourable. If it's too thick, you can add a little milk or water to reach the desired consistency.
3. **Heat the Oil:**
    - Heat about 1/2 inch of oil in a large skillet or frying pan over medium heat. Test the oil temperature by dropping a small amount of batter into the oil; it should sizzle and float to the top.
4. **Fry the Fritters:**
    - Drop spoonfuls of batter into the hot oil, flattening them slightly with the back of the spoon to form small pancakes.
    - Fry the fritters for 2-3 minutes per side, or until golden brown and cooked through. Be careful not to overcrowd the pan; fry in batches if necessary.
    - Remove the fritters from the oil with a slotted spoon and drain them on paper towels.
5. **Serve:**
    - Serve the plantain fritters warm. They can be enjoyed on their own or with a variety of toppings or dips, such as honey, yogurt, or a sprinkle of powdered sugar for a sweet treat, or a sprinkle of salt and a side of salsa for a savory option.

Tips

- **Plantain Ripeness:** Make sure the plantains are ripe but not overripe. Overripe plantains can become too soft and may not hold together well during frying.
- **Texture:** If you prefer a smoother batter, blend the plantain mixture thoroughly. For a chunkier texture, mash the plantains by hand.
- **Oil Temperature:** Maintain the oil temperature at medium heat to ensure the fritters cook evenly without burning.

Plantain Fritters are a delightful treat that can be adapted to your taste preferences. Whether you enjoy them sweet or savory, they offer a crispy exterior and a soft, flavorful interior that's sure to please. Enjoy!

Strawberry Horchata Popsicles

Ingredients

For the Horchata Base:

- **1 cup rice** (short-grain or medium-grain)
- **2 cups water**
- **1 can (12 oz) evaporated milk**
- **1 can (14 oz) sweetened condensed milk**
- **1/2 cup milk** (whole milk or any milk of choice)
- **1 tablespoon vanilla extract**
- **1 teaspoon ground cinnamon**
- **Pinch of salt**

For the Strawberry Mixture:

- **2 cups fresh strawberries** (hulled and sliced)
- **1/4 cup granulated sugar** (adjust based on the sweetness of the strawberries)
- **1 tablespoon lemon juice** (optional, to balance the flavors)

Instructions

1. **Prepare the Horchata Base:**
   - Rinse the rice under cold water until the water runs clear.
   - In a medium saucepan, combine the rinsed rice and 2 cups of water. Bring to a boil, then reduce the heat to low and simmer, covered, for about 15-20 minutes, or until the rice is tender and the water is absorbed.
   - Allow the rice to cool slightly, then transfer it to a blender or food processor. Blend with 1 cup of milk until smooth.
   - In a large bowl, combine the rice mixture with evaporated milk, sweetened condensed milk, additional milk, vanilla extract, ground cinnamon, and a pinch of salt. Stir until well combined.
2. **Prepare the Strawberry Mixture:**
   - In a blender or food processor, combine the sliced strawberries, granulated sugar, and lemon juice (if using). Blend until smooth.
   - Taste and adjust the sweetness if needed by adding more sugar.
3. **Assemble the Popsicles:**
   - Pour the horchata mixture into popsicle molds, filling them about halfway.
   - Spoon a layer of strawberry mixture on top of the horchata mixture in each mold.
   - Use a toothpick or skewer to gently swirl the strawberry mixture into the horchata mixture for a marbled effect.
4. **Insert Sticks and Freeze:**

- Insert popsicle sticks into the molds.
- Freeze the popsicles for at least 4-6 hours, or until completely frozen.

5. **Unmold and Serve:**
   - To release the popsicles from the molds, run warm water over the outside of the molds for a few seconds.
   - Gently pull the popsicles out of the molds.

Tips

- **Swirling:** For a more pronounced swirl, don't mix the strawberry and horchata mixtures too thoroughly. Just swirl lightly.
- **Rice Texture:** Ensure the rice is well-blended to avoid a gritty texture in the horchata base.
- **Mold Size:** If using small popsicle molds, adjust the freezing time as needed. Smaller molds will freeze faster.

Strawberry Horchata Popsicles offer a creamy, fruity, and refreshing combination of flavors that are perfect for cooling down on a warm day. Enjoy these homemade treats with friends and family for a delicious and unique dessert!

www.ingramcontent.com/pod-product-compliance
Lightning Source LLC
LaVergne TN
LVHW081558060526
838201LV00054B/1957